Schools, Pupils and Special Educational Needs

DAVID GALLOWAY

CROOM HELM
London • Sydney • Wolfeboro, New Hampshire

© 1985 David Galloway
Croom Helm Ltd, Provident House, Burrell Row,
Beckenham, Kent, BR3 1AT

Croom Helm Australia, 44-50 Waterloo Road,
North Ryde, 2113, New South Wales

Reprinted 1987

British Library Cataloguing in Publication Data

Galloway, David M.
    Schools , pupils and special educational needs.
    1. Exceptional children — Education — England
    I. Title
    371.9′0942   LC3986.G7

    ISBN 0-7099-1160-2
    ISBN 0-7099-1175-0 Pbk

Croom Helm, 27 South Main Street,
Wolfeboro, New Hampshire 03894-2069, USA

Library of Congress Cataloging in Publication Data

Galloway, David.
    Schools, pupils, and special educational needs.
    Includes index.
    1. Problem children — Education — England — Sheffield
(South Yorkshire) 2. Problem children — Education — New
Zealand. 3. Learning disabilities — England — Sheffield
(South Yorkshire) 4. Learning disabilities — New Zealand.
I. Title.
LC4803.G72S464 1985   371.93   84-23077
ISBN 0-7099-1160-2
ISBN 0-7099-1175-0 (pbk.)

Printed and bound in Great Britain by
Biddles Ltd, Guildford and King's Lynn

CONTENTS

ACKNOWLEDGEMENTS

This book draws on research carried out in Sheffield, England, and in New Zealand. The research in Sheffield was funded by the Department of Education and Science, whose support is gratefully acknowledged. I am also grateful for their support and advice to Mr G.M.A. Harrison, chief education officer in Sheffield, Mr David Loxley, principal psychologist, Mr Brian Wilcox, senior advisor, and Professor John Roach, Professor of Education at the University of Sheffield. The research in New Zealand was funded by the New Zealand Education Department, the New Zealand Educational Institute and the Mental Health Foundation of New Zealand. Their support also is gratefully acknowledged. Finally, I am grateful to the numerous but necessarily anonymous schools, teachers, other professional colleagues, pupils and parents whose co-operation helped me to formulate the ideas in this book.

The first draft of this book was read by Mrs Arlene Ramasut, lecturer in education at University College, Cardiff. Her comments undoubtedly improved the book, but she has no responsibility for its shortcomings.

INTRODUCTION

Background

It is now nearly seven years since the committee chaired by Mary Warnock produced its report 'Special Educational Needs' (DES, 1978). The report was the first in the history of British education to attempt a comprehensive analysis of the special education field. Many of the committee's assumptions have been challenged. Some of its detailed recommendations have been criticised. The report has, however, unquestionably led to unprecedented public discussion about children's special needs and how they may best be met. As a consciousness raising exercise the report has been outstandingly successful.

The government's response to the Warnock Report has been the 1981 Education Act. It places wide-ranging responsibilities on local education authorities (l.e.a.'s), school governors and teachers. It also gives parents extensive opportunity to share in educational decisions about their children.

Much progress has undoubtedly been achieved. Many special schools are extending their curriculum and developing constructive links with neighbouring primary or secondary schools. Special schools are less frequently a 'life sentence', with no practical possibility of return to the mainstream, than was once the case. Increasingly, primary and secondary schools are recognising the range and complexity of their children's special needs and allocating more resources to them.

Areas of unease are not, however, difficult to find. At least 90 per cent of all children who were considered by Mary Warnock's committee to have special educational needs have always been taught in ordinary schools. Yet much of the debate in the last few years has focused on the small minority who are placed in separate special schools or integrated into ordinary schools as a result of l.e.a. policy or parental insistence. More seriously, when debate has centred on ordinary schools it has frequently been confined to fairly basic descriptions of specific projects. Such descriptions are both necessary and useful. Their limitation is that they have generally paid insufficient attention to the wider context in which the projects take place. As a result, they have been so busy describing how children's needs are being met that they have often failed to discuss how the school itself might have exacerbated, or even created, those same needs.

When working in a residential school for maladjusted children I suspected that the school was having a harmful effect on as many children as it helped. Ordinary schools, too, can provide experiences which are potentially damaging to some pupils. Most educational psychologists find that schools vary widely in the sort of pupil they refer for advice. Some refer mainly disruptive pupils, others mainly children with learning problems, others pupils with emotional or family problems. Working as an educational psychologist, I at first thought that this reflected referral bias; in other words, all schools contained children with a wide range of problems, but decisions about referral depended on the skills and priorities of the school's teachers. It gradually became clear that this view was incorrect. Some schools were plagued by disruptive behaviour. Others, serving similar or more disadvantaged catchment areas, were not. Some schools had large numbers of severely under-achieving pupils. Others did not. Thus, whether a child gave evidence of having special educational needs depended at least in part on which school he happened to be attending.

Subsequent research on truancy and disruptive behaviour in schools confirmed that there were in fact differences between schools which greatly influenced the quality of education the schools offered their most difficult or backward pupils. Not surprisingly, these differences were also reflected in the teachers' feelings about their work. Further studies, carried out in New Zealand, on responses to disruptive pupils and on stress and satisfaction in teaching helped to elucidate the relationship between teachers' and pupils' experiences of school.

It gradually became clear, then, that teachers as individuals and schools as organisations often played an important part in the development of children's special educational needs. It became equally clear that the children's needs were intricately linked to those of their teachers. These conclusions reflect some of the underlying assumptions on which this book is based.

Underlying Assumptions

These can be stated concisely:

(1) *Children* are seen as having special educational needs when their *teachers* are disturbed by their progress or by their behaviour. Hence, it makes no sense to see children's needs in isolation from those of their teachers.

(2) Teachers in ordinary schools can, and do, cater successfully for children with a wide and complex range of needs. This is not, however, so likely when the children are taught in 'remedial' or separate special classes, for reasons which the book discusses in detail. Needs identified in the ordinary class are, generally, most effectively met there.

(3) Schools are also able to aggravate, if not create, the problems which are taken as evidence of special needs.

(4) The fact that a child has special needs does not necessarily imply that the child, as an individual, needs help. The most effective way to help the child may be to review aspects of school organisation, or teaching methods and resources.

(5) A child's special needs are more likely to be met, with a consequent feeling for the teacher of satisfaction, if the child is seen primarily as a teaching problem, rather than as having a learning or behaviour problem. Seeing the child as a teaching problem implies that teachers see it is their responsibility to teach him. In contrast, when he is seen as a learning or behaviour problem the implication is that the problem resides 'in' the child, and is therefore not the teacher's responsibility. A characteristic of some of the most successful schools we studied was that class and subject teachers did not transfer to specialists responsibility for their pupils with special needs.

Scope

The book is concerned mainly with pupils who have special needs, but who would not normally be regarded as candidates for separate special schools or classes. In other words, the book is concerned with the majority of pupils regarded by the Warnock committee as having special needs. In very broad terms these pupils are educationally backward, have specific learning difficulties or present some form of behavioural problem. They therefore constitute a highly varied group, presenting a wide and complex range of problems with which all experienced teachers will be familiar.

This book does not discuss the needs of children with sensory or physical disabilities. Nor is it primarily concerned with the question whether slow-learning and so-called maladjusted children should be educated in special schools or ordinary schools. It does, however, consider in some detail the effects on ordinary schools of the separate special school system, arguing that these are mostly adverse. This means that the overlapping needs of children in ordinary and in special schools are discussed at various stages. Some special schools certainly offer a high quality of education. Just as certainly, some ordinary schools also cater most effectively for their pupils with special needs. Quite consistently the research evidence favours ordinary schools. The integration-segregation debate is discussed elsewhere (Galloway and Goodwin, 1979). This book is concerned principally with the ordinary school system.

Except in passing, the book makes no attempt to describe techniques of assessment nor to discuss the details of individual or group programmes designed to meet special needs. The reason may be depressing but it is at least straightforward. HMI reports, both in Scotland and in England and Wales, imply quite clearly that most teachers with responsibility for special needs have neither the training nor the experience to plan individual programmes utilising the results of a comprehensive and detailed assessment. Even if they had the training and experience, the majority would not have the time, given existing teaching loads. Even if they had the time to plan individualised programmes, they would seldom have the opportunity to use them given existing class sizes. Probably the most bizarre aspect of special education is the time and energy spent on highly complex assessment techniques, the results of which are frequently of minimal practical value to teachers. Yet against all this, there is good evidence that teachers in ordinary schools can cater effectively for pupils with special needs, even though the children's curriculum is very seldom based on the results of elaborate, complex psychological assessment techniques.

This book is concerned with much broader but, in my view, neglected issues of l.e.a. policy, school organisation and classroom practice. These broader issues determine the attitudes of teachers towards pupils with special needs. These issues reflect, and are reflected in the professional development of teachers, and determine the quality of education they are able to offer their more vulnerable pupils.

Organisation and Aims

Chapter 1 deals with the definition and meaning of special educational needs, and with the practical implications for classroom teachers. The likely impact of the 1981 Education Act on classroom practice and on the work of the educational support services is covered in Chapter 2. The vexed issue of assessment and 'Statementing' — the awful neologism arising from the 1981 Act — is discussed in Chapter 3, which is followed by chapters dealing successively with school-based policy and provision for children with special needs, and with responses to disturbing behaviour. The next two chapters discuss the role of the guidance network and the importance of recognising the needs of teachers themselves. The final chapter considers policy implications for schools and for l.e.a.'s.

The book draws on research into school and classroom effectiveness, educational sociology and psychology, stress and job satisfaction in teaching, as well as in special education. One aim throughout is to show how school and classroom practice can contribute to, if not create, the special educational needs which teachers may subsequently spend a lot of time trying to meet. Another aim is to show how school and classroom practice can enable teachers to identify and meet their pupils' special needs.

The legal and administrative basis for special educational provision has changed radically with the 1981 Education Act. How far this will benefit the children concerned is much less clear. Experience in related fields suggests that impressive innovations are all too easily subverted to the detriment of those they are intended to help. The present book aims to show how this may happen to the education in ordinary schools of children with special needs. It hopes to promote amongst teachers discussion and evaluation of current practice. If this enables them to meet their pupils' needs more effectively, while at the same time enhancing their own job satisfaction and professional development, the book will have succeeded.

David Galloway

1 WHOSE SPECIAL NEEDS?

Introduction

If teachers taken from a random sample in ordinary primary and secondary schools, were to be asked what they knew about the Warnock Report (DES, 1978a) almost all would know that it dealt with special education. If asked about the Report's conclusions and recommendations, there would probably be less confidence. Some might say that the report recommended the integration of handicapped children into the mainstream. They would, incidentally, be considerably over-stating the committee's position with respect to integration. The recommendation remembered by the largest number, however, might be that: 'one in six children at any one time and up to one in five children at some time in their school career will require some form of special educational provision'.

Before looking more critically at the evidence for this conclusion, and at its implications for teachers, it is worth considering the three broad areas of need which Mary Warnock and her colleagues had in mind. The first was the need for provision of special means of access to the curriculum. This applies mainly to children with physical, visual and hearing disabilities. A blind child, for example, will need to be taught braille. The second and third areas were the need for 'provision of a special or modified curriculum' and 'particular attention to the social structure and emotional climate in which education takes place'.

There is no doubt that up to 20 per cent of children have difficulty coping with the ordinary curriculum at some stage in their school lives. Nor is there much doubt that the social structure and emotional climate in the school or classroom is a source of substantial stress to a similar proportion. The question is whether a curriculum and an emotional climate which fails to cater for up to 20 per cent of pupils can be entirely suitable for the remaining 80 per cent. In more practical terms, the relationship between the proposed special or modified curriculum and the mainstream curriculum requires elucidation. This is also true of the relationship between the social structure and emotional climate needed for children with special needs and that required for 'ordinary' pupils. A recurring theme throughout this book is that special or modified curricula, and classes with special 'social structures and emotional climates' may as frequently create special needs as meet them.

Warnock's 20 per cent: Educational Reality or Statistical Fiction?

The availability of places in special schools is unevenly distributed through the country. Marked variations can even occur between neighbouring boroughs. Thus, one London borough in 1977 placed ten times more children in schools for the maladjusted than another (DES, 1978*a*). Consequently, special school places have never provided evidence about the numbers of children with special educational needs. To see how the Warnock Committee formed its conclusions we have to look at evidence from studies of larger groups of children.

Disturbing Behaviour

The most widely quoted investigations are the National Child Development Study, and those carried out by Professor Michael Rutter and his colleagues on the Isle of Wight and in an Inner London borough. The National Child Development Study included all children born between 3rd and 9th March, 1958. On the basis of the teacher version of Stott's Bristol Social Adjustment Guide (1963), 64 per cent of children were rated as stable, 22 per cent as unsettled and 14 per cent as maladjusted (Davie *et al.*, 1972). The same study showed that 13 per cent of children were thought by teachers to need special educational help, but only 5 per cent were in fact receiving it.

Rutter and his colleagues asked teachers to complete a behaviour questionnaire (Rutter, 1967) on the pupils they studied. In addition they interviewed the children's mothers, and on the Isle of Wight, but not in London, the children themselves. 19 per cent of children were rated as deviant in the Inner London borough on the basis of the teacher's questionnaire results, compared with 11 per cent in the Isle of Wight. Using all the available questionnaire and interview data, 25 per cent of London's 10-year-olds were said to be showing 'clinically significant' signs of psychiatric disorder, compared with 12 per cent on the Isle of Wight. The term psychiatric disorder was used to include 'abnormalities of emotions, behaviour or relationships which are developmentally inappropriate, and of sufficient duration and severity to cause persistent suffering or handicap to the child and/or distress or disturbance to the family or community' (Rutter and Graham, 1968).

An interesting incidental observation from the Isle of Wight study was the small overlap between children whose parents were concerned about their behaviour and children whose teachers expressed concern (Rutter *et al.*, 1970). This was partly attributable to teachers reporting more behaviour problems of a broadly antisocial type, while parents tended to report a larger number of withdrawn children. Children whose parents complain about their behaviour at home may have special needs. Whether they have special *educational* needs is another question altogether.

Two explanation may be put forward for the low overlap between behaviour problems at home and at school, as reported by parents and teachers. One is that parents and teachers interpret similar behaviour in different ways. 'Quietness', for example, may be considered a virtue by some teachers who may be more concerned about openly disruptive pupils. Parents, on the other hand, may see quietness as an indication of lack of confidence or of anxiety in social situations. Another explanation is that children behave in different ways in different contexts.

Both explanations are valid. Both draw attention to the teacher's role in attributing special educational needs to a child. Teachers vary between themselves in how they interpret behaviour. A healthy extrovert to one teacher can be a thoroughly noisy, disruptive nuisance to another. Similarly the child that one teacher in an open plan class sees as quiet, but sensitive and creative, may be seen as an immature, withdrawn little baby by another. Disturbing classroom behaviour, in other words, is not a problem because of any objective criteria in the behaviour itself, but rather because of the effect it has on teachers.

All experienced teachers, moreover, will recall children whose behaviour has changed dramatically with a change of teacher. In the same way a change of school can be accompanied by a change of attitudes and of behaviour. At home, parents recognise that their children's language changes according to the company they are in; expressions and pronunciation considered unacceptable within the family may be necessary for social acceptance in the street or the playground. Thus, a teacher's statement that a child's behaviour indicates a need for special educational help has to be seen in terms not only of the teacher's own values and attitudes, but also in terms of the child's behaviour in a particular context.

An observation from a follow-up to the Isle of Wight study revealed a slight increase in the prevalence of psychiatric disorder at age 14 compared with four years earlier (Rutter *et al.*, 1976). This was not, however, attributable to any important increase in the rate of overtly disruptive behaviour of most immediate concern to teachers. More important, perhaps, just over half the pupils assessed as showing signs of psychiatric disorder had first presented problems as adolescents. Fewer than half had been disturbing their parents or teachers four years earlier. This observation has two implications. Firstly, as the Warnock report recognised, the problems presented by many pupils are transient. Secondly, concentrating provision for pupils with special needs on the younger age-groups would be of limited value, even if all the pupils concerned could be 'treated' successfully. This is not the case, nor is there any way of identifying reliably pupils who will disturb their teachers towards the end of their school careers. Even if these pupils *could* be identified, there would be no way of telling what their educational needs would be, let alone how they should be met. We shall return later in the chapter to the confusion surrounding the concept of special educational need on account of disturbing behaviour. Firstly, though, we need to look at the prevalence of learning difficulties.

Learning Difficulties

Nationally, special schools for pupils with moderate learning difficulties, formerly known as ESN(M), account for roughly 1 per cent of school age pupils. This tells us nothing, however, about the number of children who might be experiencing learning difficulties. To see why, we need to consider the range of problems subsumed under the blanket term learning difficulties.

The 1944 Education Act and subsequent regulations (Ministry of Education, 1945) did not define criteria for ascertainment as ESN. Subsequent publications, though, made clear that special schools for ESN pupils should cater predominantly for those with a low IQ, generally assessed as below 70 or 75 (Ministry of Education, 1958, 1961). We shall return to the uses of IQ tests shortly. The point here is that the controversy was associated with two questions:

(1) The way in which most IQ tests are constructed ensures that roughly 2.5 per cent of the population will obtain a score below 70.

(2) Virtually all special schools for children with moderate learning difficulties have always admitted a disproportionate
number of boys and a substantial minority of pupils with
relatively high measured intelligence (Ministry of Education,
1958). Further, they have in many areas aroused understandable anger and suspicion by admitting a disproportionate
number of children of Caribbean origin (e.g. Coard, 1971).
The implication is that they have been used as convenient
places for problem pupils, and not simply as the most appropriate place in which to meet the needs of pupils with
moderate learning difficulties.

Even without the confusion surrounding criteria for admission to
a special school for children with moderate learning difficulties we
would still be no nearer an idea of the prevalence of learning difficulties. The predicted figure of about 2.5 per cent scoring below 70
on an IQ test is a purely statistical artifact of the way most of these
tests are constructed, a point to which we return shortly. We
therefore need to look at the number of children believed to have
learning difficulties in ordinary schools.

Yule *et al.* (1974) noted that 8 per cent of 10-year-olds in the Isle
of Wight and 19 per cent in an Inner London borough had a
reading age at least 28 months below their chronological age. In
most cases the poor reading ability was associated with low
measured intelligence. In other words, their reading level could be
predicted from knowledge of their IQ. These pupils were regarded
as backward readers. Nearly 3 per cent of the Isle of Wight pupils
and 10 per cent of the London pupils were reading significantly
below the level predicted by their age and IQ. These pupils with
specific reading retardation overlapped with the backward group.
Their special educational needs, though, were more specifically
confined to reading, since they did not, on the whole, have similar
problems in mathematics.

Multiple 'Handicap'

The four criteria noted so far in defining learning difficulties which
indicate special educational need are an IQ below 70, reading
backwardness, specific reading retardation and psychiatric
disorder. At least one of these conditions applied to 16 per cent of
10-year-olds on the Isle of Wight (Rutter *et al.*, 1970). More than

one condition applied to a quarter of this 16 per cent, or 4 per cent of the total.

Warnock refers to these criteria as 'handicaps'. Certainly, they have been taken as evidence both in the report and in subsequent discussion, as evidence of special educational need. It is therefore worth asking whether there was anything in the least surprising in the evidence that up to 20 per cent of children may have special educational needs, as defined in the report, at some stage in their school career. It is also worth asking whether the criteria themselves can meaningfully be seen as valid.

Prevalence of Special Educational Needs: a Critique

Neither New, Nor Surprising

The first thing to be said about Warnock's conclusion on the prevalence of special educational need is that it could equally well have been reached on adequate research evidence at any time in the previous 50 years. This is true both of pupils whose behaviour disturbs their teachers and of children with learning difficulties.

As early as 1925 Haggerty had found teachers in North America reporting undesirable behaviour in more than 50 per cent of pupils. In London elementary schools teachers reported one or more of four 'behaviour deviations' in 46 per cent of pupils (McFie, 1934). The 'deviations' listed were timidity or lack of sociability, behaviour disorders such as truancy or stealing, habit disorders such as nail-biting or incontinence, and educational problems not attributable to mental deficiency. In the private sector, teachers at five schools run by the Girls Public Day Schools Trust had put forward 17 per cent of pupils for interview on account of difficult behaviour (Milner, 1938). Other studies, in North America, had been reviewed by Uger (1938) with broadly similar results.

The position on children with learning difficulties was equally clear. Cyril Burt's (1937) book *The Backward Child*, written in his early years when his probity as a researcher remains relatively unquestioned is regarded as a classic. In it he concluded that one child in ten above the 'educable defective' level was backward, and only one in six of the so-called educable defectives, later labelled ESN(M), was actually in a special school. These pupils, moreover were 'lacking not so much in social capacity as in scholastic capacity, they are incompetent pupils rather than incapable citizens'. Yet even earlier than this the first Medical Inspection to the Education Department had described as 'very numerous' children requiring special education because they are 'physically and morally healthy — but backward'.

Burt himself exerted a strong influence on the deliberations between 1924 – 29 of a committee chaired by A.H. Wood into the educational needs of the 'feeble-minded'. Excluding children with severe learning difficulties, who were then outside the education system altogether, the committee considered that existing special schools catered for only one-sixth of the estimated number of feeble minded children in the country. These children, formerly known as ESN(M), would today be said to have moderate learning difficulties. In addition, the Committee noted the special needs of children who did not formally qualify as feeble minded, estimating that they included roughly a further 10 per cent of the population (Board of Education and Board of Control, 1929).

A Statistical Fiction?

Tests of intelligence and of educational attainments are designed to assess children with a wide range of ability. Most intelligence tests are designed with a mean of 100 and a standard deviation of 15. The sample on which the norms are based is assumed to be representative of the population as a whole. Hence the design of the test ensures that roughly 34 per cent of children will obtain scores between 85 – 100 (within one standard deviation below the mean), and more than 47 per cent between 70 – 100 (within two standard deviations below the mean).

Results of reading tests are more frequently described in terms of reading ages. Thus a child who has a reading age of 10 on his tenth birthday is reading 'up to' his chronological age. For statistical reasons reading quotients derived from the chronological age are misleading (Yule, 1973), particularly at the extremes.

If the way the tests are constructed ensures a wide range of scores, care is obviously necessary in using the results as evidence of special educational needs. Is it, for example, legitimate to regard as handicapped, and hence in need of special educational help, children whose low reading age is wholly predictable from evidence on their intellectual ability? The Warnock Committee could argue that a reading age 28 months below chronological age indicates a need for special help. This would be a reasonable reply, but evades an important part of the problem, that is, that the cut-off point of 28 months is an arbitrary one.

Purely from a research point of view, it is both legitimate and necessary to define some arbitrary criterion of backwardness. Without some such criterion it is logically impossible to report the number of pupils falling below the criterion. Yet in implicitly using the researchers' criterion to define special educational need, thus going further than the researchers themselves, the Committee was making an essentially moral, and political, judgement about the children that teachers in ordinary classes should, or should not, be expected to teach without additional help.

This point becomes clearer by considering different criteria the committee might have accepted. Its members could have regarded any child with a reading age more than 18 months behind his chronological age as having special educational needs. Had they done so, the proportion thought to require special help would have been much higher. Alternatively, they could have accepted 36 months backwardness as indicating a need for special help. In this case the proportion would have been considerably lower. What the Committee in effect seemed to do was to think of a percentage point, and assert that any child falling below this point had special needs. The corollary, of course, was that the teachers of any child falling below the specified level needed special help in order to meet the child's needs. The wide range of scores guaranteed by the method of constructing intelligence and reading tests could then be relied on to provide educational justification for the political decision. This problem cannot be evaded by claiming that 28 months is the stage at which *teachers* think they need special help, since that depends on the average for the class, on the teachers' experience and on their expectations of what the children 'ought' to be achieving.

A similar problem is evident in ascribing special educational need on behavioural grounds. The evidence summarised above, and by Galloway *et al.* (1982*a*) lends no support to the widespread belief that behaviour problems are on the increase. Teachers have always expressed concern about a substantial minority of their pupils, and probably always will. In a competitive, achievement orientated society, the lowest achievers and the least conforming pupils will inevitably be regarded as problems. The concepts of underachievement and disturbing, or, more speculatively, 'disturbed' behaviour, have no meaning without reference to some agreed norm. Children can be said to underachieve or overachieve with reference to their measured intelligence. The reference point cannot, however, logically be their chronological age since that would imply the logical impossibility of raising everyone to an average level — the point being that the average would change as overall standards improved. In the case of behaviour, the norm can only be the teacher's or researcher's, view on what behaviour should be considered acceptable or unacceptable.

The instruments used in most of the research on children's behaviour on which the Warnock Committee based its conclusions were the Rutter A_2 Scale (Rutter, 1967) and Denis Stott's Bristol Social Adjustment Guides (Stott, 1963, 1971). Rutter's Scale contains 26 items seen as possible symptoms of psychiatric disorder, for example, 'restless, cannot remain seated for long', or 'often has temper tantrums'. The teacher has to state whether each item definitely applies, applies somewhat, or does not apply. Stott's Guides are longer, and require teachers to underline statements that apply to the child in question. Rutter's Scale is essentially a screening instrument designed to identify children who would be regarded as showing 'clinically significant' signs of psychiatric disorder in an interview with a psychiatrist. Stott's Guides aim to identify children who could be considered maladjusted and to describe the nature of their problems. They aim to give teachers more clinical information than Rutter's Scale, though their usefulness has been strongly challenged (e.g. Yule, 1976).

Both instruments depend for their popularity and their success on containing items which are familiar to teachers. If they contained problems which were *not* familiar to teachers, they would be open to criticism on at least three grounds:

(1) Nil returns are of very limited interest, either to teachers or to researchers.
(2) Teachers would rapidly become bored with completing the forms.
(3) Teachers would quite reasonably feel that the researchers were insensitive to, or unaware of, the problems in children's behaviour which most concerned them.

Yet by including items which *are* familiar to teachers, both instruments prejudge the issue: they ensure that a substantial minority of children will be regarded as deviant, maladjusted, disturbed or just disturbing, depending on the preferred label.

Surveys of children's behaviour are therefore open to exactly the same criticism as the results of intelligence and attainment tests. Moreover the Warnock Committee's interpretation of the results is just as political. In the case of children with learning difficulties, the Committee had to decide what proportion of children whose progress deviated from some arbitrary, and rather ill-defined, concept of normality could reasonably be considered to have special educational needs. In the case of behaviour problems the question was what proportion of children whose behaviour deviated from some equally arbitrary and equally ill-defined concept of normality could reasonably be considered to have special educational needs. Having decided on a proportion, the research evidence was at hand to justify the conclusion.

It needs to be said that there is no evidence that the Committee did in fact approach the question in the cynical way suggested here. Our analysis aims rather to demonstrate that the evidence on the prevalence of special educational needs is open to more than one interpretation. By attributing special needs to 20 per cent of the population the Committee was not simply drawing attention to the needs of a minority. As the report quite clearly recognised, drawing attention to these children's needs carried a clear implication that something should be done about them. Since the majority were, and would remain, in ordinary schools, it followed that most special educational needs would have to be met in ordinary schools. Unfortunately, there could be no guarantee that some procedures adopted to meet the alleged needs would avoid the worst faults of segregated special schools.

What Needs?

When a teacher becomes concerned about a child's progress or behaviour an initial response is to ask whether anything in his medical history or family background throws light on the problem. As far as it goes this is reasonable. Although the overlap between behaviour problems at home and at school is small (Rutter *et al.*, 1970) it is unreasonable to expect that feelings of stress about a situation at home will have no effect on a child's progress or behaviour at school. The obvious corollary, which it is all too easy for teachers to overlook, is that stress at school may well affect a child's behaviour at home. Thus, disturbing behaviour or lack of progress at school can readily be attributed to problems at home.

Yet if a parent seeks advice about behaviour problems at home, the immediate temptation may be to assume that the parent's handling of the child is at fault. In either event, parents are held responsible, implicitly exonerating teachers.

The Warnock Report referred to special *educational* needs. It makes clear, however, that teachers cannot meet these needs on their own. One chapter is devoted to co-operation with parents — 'Parents as Partners' and the question of inter-professional co-operation is dealt with at length in other chapters. The report is generally optimistic about the ability of teachers to meet their pupil's special needs. A question which it largely overlooks is whether the inter-professional co-operation which it advocates may successfully identify personal and family problems, but obscure much more relevant needs created by the curriculum and in the educational climate. Before turning to the school's influence on children's behaviour and educational progress, though, we need to consider individual, family and social influences.

Children Presenting Behaviour Problems

The children who showed 'clinically significant' signs of psychiatric disorder in the Isle of Wight and Inner London borough studies had, or presented, quite serious problems. As noted earlier their problems were 'of sufficient duration and severity to cause persistent suffering or handicap to the child and/or distress or disturbance to the family or community' (Rutter and Graham, 1968). Another way of expressing this is that the children were themselves experiencing considerable stress. Several points, though, remain unclear. Warnock regarded children who met Rutter and Graham's criterion of psychiatric disorder as having special needs. Later in the chapter we discuss the troublesome question of whose needs we are talking about. Does it make sense to talk about children having special needs when adults are distressed or disturbed by their behaviour? At this stage we need only note that many, though by no means all, children regarded as having special educational needs on account of their behaviour are themselves experiencing 'persistent suffering or handicap'. That, however, tells us little about the children under discussion.

Social Class

Behavioural problems and moderate educational subnormality, (maladjusted and ESN(M) pupils in the old terminology), were alone amongst the former categories of handicap (Ministry of Education, 1959) to have a skewed social class distribution. In other words, children in other categories came from all social classes in roughly the proportion predicted from the general population. In contrast, children with behavioural and learning problems tended to come from working class homes.

Detailed discussion of research into the relationship between social class and educational achievement is beyond the scope of this book. Conflicting theories about social class differences, such as those of Bernstein (1971) and Labov (1970) on uses of language, do, however, give us clues as to how working class pupils may be disadvantaged in the school system. The fact that they are at a disadvantage, consistently performing less well than their peers from middle class homes, is not in dispute. To the extent that factors related to social class contribute to differences in educational attainment they are relevant to an analysis of special educational needs.

Social Disadvantage

In their analysis of data from the National Child Development Study, Wedge and Prosser (1973) identified 4.5 per cent of 11-year-olds as disadvantaged. The criteria for identifying these children were that their families:

(1) had only one parent and/or five or more children,
and
(2) lived in an over-crowded house or a house with no hot water,
and
(3) were in receipt of means tested welfare benefits on account of their low income.

By the age of 16 2.9 per cent were disadvantaged on these criteria (Wedge and Essen, 1982).

The surveys showed a strong relationship between disadvantage and educational attainment. Moreover, the relationship became more marked during adolescence. At the very least the results suggest that children living in disadvantaged circumstances are more likely than other children to meet Warnock's criteria of special educational need.

Family Disadvantage

Generalisations about potentially stressful events such as parental separation or divorce invite contradiction. Thus, the effect of parental separation is likely to depend largely on what happens in the family subsequently. Rutter *et al.* (1975) showed that London children whose parents had separated or divorced were more likely to show behavioural problems than children on the Isle of Wight. This was probably because a much higher proportion of the Isle of Wight parents had married again, in most cases happily.

To take another example, illness in one or both parents is associated with a high rate of problem behaviour in the children (Rutter, 1966), mental illness appearing to be a greater risk factor than physical illness. On the other hand, in London psychiatric disorder in the mother was less frequently associated with psychiatric disorder in the child than in the Isle of Wight (Rutter *et al.*, 1975). In Sheffield Galloway (1982*a*) found a high rate of psychiatric disorder, mainly depression, in parents of persistent absentees from an inner city secondary school. The relationship between performance at school and poor parental health nevertheless remains an open question.

What is not in doubt, however, is that some children live in conditions which they find acutely stressful. It does not follow that removing them from home would help them, since reception into the care of a local authority can itself be educationally and emotionally disruptive (e.g. Tutt, 1981; Sutton, 1978). Nor does it follow that disadvantage in the home will necessarily be reflected in a child's behaviour at school.

'Vulnerable' Children

Children can be vulnerable by reason of adverse circumstances at home or at school. They can also be vulnerable by reason of personal factors. Slow progress can result from inadequate teaching. It can also result from low intelligence or from developmental delay in some specific area, for example certain language or perceptual skills required in the early stages of reading.

Medical or constitutional factors may also contribute to the likelihood of some pupils behaving in an anti-social manner. The relationship between temporal lobe epilepsy and behaviour problems has been investigated extensively with inconclusive results (Harris, 1978; Kligman and Goldberg, 1975). The relationship between food allergies and over-active behaviour has also attracted extensive attention, though Cantwell (1977) has argued that none of the claims has been substantiated. A sample of pupils suspended from school for disruptive behaviour was found to have had a high rate of serious illnesses or accidents compared with their siblings. These pupils were also more likely than their siblings to have been in care (Galloway, 1982*b*). The causal relationship is perhaps only of academic interest: they might have had illnesses and accidents and have been placed in care, because they were vulnerable, or vice versa. The point is that their medical histories could, at least, be seen as associated to some extent with the problems they presented at school.

Comment

So far we have merely identified some social, family and personal characteristics commonly found in pupils regarded as having special educational needs. The list is certainly not intended to be comprehensive. Rather it aims to show that:

(1) Many children have special needs, even though these may not necessarily constitute educational needs.
(2) These needs arise from a range of personal, family and social circumstances.

Three further points should be made at this stage.

(1) There is evidence that children can cope quite successfully with stressful situations if these are isolated, (e.g. Rutter, 1978). Problems arise when stress is experienced from several sources interacting with and aggravating each other. A child may be able to cope with overcrowding, or friction between parents, or a sick parent, but not, perhaps, with all three. In Sheffield we found that persistent absentees from a secondary school came from multiply disadvantaged families compared with regular attenders of the same age and sex and from the same class in school (Galloway, 1982*b*).
(2) The connection between social disadvantage and educational disadvantage is by no means straightforward. There is clearly no justification for regarding a child as having special educational needs on social grounds alone. We know that both social disadvantage and a combination of stresses within the

family are associated with an increased risk of problems at school which would bring a child into Warnock's 20 per cent. Yet this tells us nothing about the ways in which a child's experiences at home may affect his behaviour and progress at school. Nor, of course, does it give any suggestion as to how experiences at school may affect his tolerance of adverse circumstances at home. The third point develops from this.

(3) So far we have said nothing about the school's influence on children's behaviour and progress. If teachers themselves exert an influence over their pupil's behaviour and progress independent of the social background, it follows logically that they may have considerable responsibility for creating, or preventing the problems associated with special educational need. Moreover, experiences of stress at school, for example through repeated failure in the curriculum, are likely to compound and aggravate experiences of stress at home. As we saw earlier, a combination of stresses has much more serious consequences than single ones. Conversely, experience of success and satisfaction at school may help a child to cope with adverse conditions at home. We must now consider this possibility.

The School's Influence on Behaviour and Progress

Underlying Assumptions

The Warnock Report referred to parents as partners with teachers in their children's education. Almost all head teachers accept this view in theory but very few reflect it in practice. All too often the 'partnership' is confined to parental involvement in non-professional activities such as fund-raising, the termly, or annual, parents' evening, and a willingness to discuss 'problems' with parents as and when requested.

It is now well-established that parents' involvement when a child is learning to read has a major effect on the child's progress (Hewison and Tizard, 1980; Tizard *et al.*, 1982), far greater than extra or 'remedial' help from teachers at school. This research incidentally, was carried out in a disadvantaged area of London. It is not just middle-class parents who can help their children.

Yet no more than a tiny minority of primary schools throughout the country seeks parental co-operation in the planned way that has been found effective. An even tinier minority encourages parents to help in the classroom in the way that is now taken for granted in other countries such as Sweden and New Zealand. The overwhelming majority appear to believe that teaching is an activity best carried out between teachers and consenting children in the decent privacy of the classroom. If the child has problems, then this calls for extra help from the teacher professionals rather than for a review of ways that professionals and parents can work together.

Insisting on the teacher's exclusive competence to teach effectively excludes the parent, or ensures that any parental help is given, at best, in parallel with that of the school. It is a short step from here for teachers to see themselves as compensating for unsatisfactory home-backgrounds. Unfortunately there is a catch here.

If teachers see their own activities as being, by definition, in the child's best interests, it becomes difficult, logically, to evaluate these activities. Excellence, after all, implies, and hence does not require evaluation. If schools are seen as compensating for inadequacies in the home, then educational failure, and related problems such as truancy and maladjustment, must also be seen as originating in the home. At best, some schools may be more effective in compensating for home background than others.

This view has been held by eminent educationists. It lay behind the Plowden Report recommendation to establish educational priority areas (DES, 1967). The rationale was that a child's progress and behaviour depended partly on the child's own intelligence and personality, largely on the family and social background, and scarcely at all on the school. Since nothing could be done about the family and social background, the only hope lay in extra 'compensatory' experience at school. At the time there seemed to be overwhelming evidence for this thesis, mainly from the Coleman Report in America (Coleman *et al.*, 1966; Jencks, 1972).

Thus influential research in the 1960s, on which Plowden and Coleman based their findings concluded that schools made little differences to their pupils' life chances. The methodological limitations which led to this conclusion have been discussed elsewhere (e.g. Rutter *et al.*, 1979; Reynolds, 1982). The issue here is that the message was an essentially negative one for teachers: more of the same might have some beneficial effect, but if there are no extra resources teachers will have little or no effect on their pupil's life chances. The message was seductive, placing responsibility for failure firmly on parents and on society. It was also a dangerous message for teachers, implying that their own training, attitude and competence were all of relatively little importance.

The alternative is at the same time more exciting, challenging and threatening. Schools as organisations and teachers as individuals may have an important influence on their pupils' progress and social adjustment. If so, schools themselves would exert an important influence on the prevalence of special educational needs. Two criteria for recognition as having special educational need are educational backwardness and seriously disturbing behaviour. How much effect does the school have on such factors?

Evidence

The first British study to claim that schools affected their pupils' behaviour was based on data from secondary schools in Tower Hamlets, London. Power *et al.* (1967, 1972) found large differences between schools in delinquency rates, and claimed that these differences could not be attributed to variations in the catchment areas. The teacher unions bitterly resented what they saw as an accusation that schools caused delinquency. Partly as a result, the research came to an abrupt halt. It would have been more helpful if the unions had recognised that Power's work also suggested that some schools prevented delinquency. His work has, however, been criticised on methodological grounds by Baldwin (1972), and other studies in London have suggested that schools with high delinquency rates tend to take pupils from catchment areas with high delinquency rates, (Farrington, 1972; West and Farrington, 1973).

In support of Power's work, Gath *et al.* (1972, 1977) noted wide variations in the number of children referred to child guidance clinics, and in the delinquency rates of London schools with similar catchment areas. Children receiving supervision or treatment from a child guidance team following referral by the school could certainly be regarded as having special educational needs. Gath's work suggests that some schools may produce more pupils than others serving similar areas.

Further support for this view comes from a study of pupils suspended from Sheffield secondary schools over a four year period (Galloway, 1980; Galloway *et al.*, 1982*a*). We found large differences between schools in the percentage of pupils suspended for disruptive behaviour. Five of the 37 schools studied accounted for roughly 50 per cent of all suspensions. Whereas catchment area characteristics could account for much of the variation between schools in persistent absentee rates, they could *not* account for the variation in suspension rates (Galloway *et al.*, 1984*a*). In other words, the differences reflected policy or practice within the schools concerned.

Suspension is the school's ultimate sanction. Any suspended pupil would certainly be regarded as having special educational needs, justifying referral to a special centre or unit, on the grounds that everything that had already been provided had proved inadequate. We should remember, of course, that the overwhelming majority of pupils regarded by Warnock as having special needs remain in ordinary schools. Yet the Sheffield evidence, together with other evidence from an anonymous l.e.a. (Grunsell, 1979, 1980) show that a pupil's chances of suspension depend mainly not on personal or family factors, but rather on which school he happens to be attending.

There is further evidence that schools exert a crucial influence on their pupils' behaviour. The 10-year-olds studied by Rutter and his colleagues in an Inner London borough were followed up at the age of 14. The behaviour of the 10-year-olds, as reported by their teachers, was used to predict with statistical techniques the number of pupils whose teachers would report deviant behaviour at 14. Rutter (1977) found that some schools reported a much higher number of pupils than had been predicted, while others reported a much lower proportion. The implication is that the number of pupils who might be said to have special educational needs because of their deviant behaviour depended on the pupil's experiences since entering the secondary school, not simply on their personal or family characteristics.

This work led to an influential study, carried out in London on school influences on pupils' performance (Rutter *et al.*, 1979). Studying 12 schools, they found marked differences in the pupils' behaviour within the school, in delinquency rates, in school attendance and in examination results. Among the most interesting results was a low correlation between their measures of the pupils when they entered secondary school and their behaviour within the school, as observed during the research. Thus, the implication here too is that pupil's behaviour at school may depend largely on factors within the school.

Research in secondary modern schools in South Wales also revealed notable differences between schools, in delinquency, attendance, and progress to further education. Again these differences could not satisfactorily be explained in terms of differences between the school catchment areas. The evidence suggested that factors within the school were playing an important part (Reynolds, 1976; Reynolds *et al.*, 1980; Reynolds and Murgatroyd, 1977).

Neither the London nor the South Wales studies investigated in detail the school's effect on those pupils with learning difficulties who might be regarded as having special educational needs. Rutter measured academic outcome by examination results and Reynolds by rates of entry to Further Education. These measures could conceal the possibility that schools exert a greater influence over the performance of their more able pupils than the less able. Rutter *et al.* (1979) checked this possibility by analysing the CSE grade four and five passes (i.e. the lowest grades which they had excluded from other analyses) for the least able group of pupils admitted to the twelve schools. Again they found substantial differences between the schools, implying that the schools were exerting an important influence on their least able pupils' progress.

This view is strengthened by re-analysis of the data collected by Coleman *et al.* (1966) from 4,000 American schools. These studies are discussed by Dyer (1968) and Reynolds (1982). They suggest that the schools may in fact have had a considerable influence as the pupils progressed through adolescence, but that this influence was only substantial on pupils of low ability or low social class and non-white pupils. These, of course, are precisely the pupils who are disproportionately represented in samples of children regarded as having special educational needs.

Comment

The argument so far can be summarised as follows:

(1) The great majority of the 20 per cent of pupils regarded by Warnock as having special educational needs remain in ordinary schools.

(2) The majority of these pupils present behavioural problems and/or learning difficulties; these latter group contains pupils of low measured intelligence and pupils whose attainments fall substantially below their chronological age, irrespective of their measured intelligence.

(3) Schools exert a very substantial influence over their pupils' behaviour; the fact that some schools have few problems from disturbed or disturbing pupil behaviour, while others are overwhelmed by problems has more to do with school factors than with factors within the catchment area.
(4) Schools also exert an important influence on their pupils' educational progress.
(5) This influence may be greatest on pupils who are least able intellectually and least privileged socially.

It is therefore tempting to conclude that special needs are created in school, by teachers; and that the number of pupils with special needs could be drastically reduced by improving the quality of teaching. Unfortunately the position is more complicated. Three reasons will be discussed here, the first of which is relatively straightforward.

Certainly, there are schools in which teachers have reason to regard very few pupils as having special needs because of their social adjustment or behaviour. Equally, there are schools in which few pupils give realistic grounds for concern on account of their academic progress. Any school with a mixed ability intake, however, will contain pupils of low measured intelligence and pupils whose attainments fall below their chronological age, even though they may not necessarily be underachieving relative to their measured intelligence. Similarly, all schools with a mixed ability intake will contain pupils requiring special attention because of personal, medical or family problems. Such pupils may be overlooked in schools with high rates of disruptive behaviour. The point is that pupils with special needs will not simply disappear because the school caters for them effectively.

Evidence that successful schools do little or nothing to reduce the range of ability among pupils is related to this. Rutter *et al.* (1979) found that the range between the most and the least able pupils was as wide in the most successful schools they studied as in the least successful. Schools, it appears, can raise the overall level of pupils' attainments, and improve the general quality of behaviour. That, however, is quite different from promoting equality. Educational equality remains a dream. However much the quality of education improves we will still be left with the disturbing 20 per cent on an academic or behavioural continuum, or 10 per cent or 30 per cent, depending on the criterion used.

Taking this point a stage further, let us suppose that all schools could reach the standards of the most successful schools described by Rutter *et al.* (1979). Clearly, scores on standard tests of educational attainment would rise, requiring publication of new 'norms' — i.e. tables enabling an individual's score to be compared with scores of the pupils on whom the test was standardised. Yet the test could still be used to identify pupils with a wide ability range. Indeed it would be designed to do precisely that.

It follows that the concept of special educational needs as conceived by the Warnock Report is logically independent of educational standards in schools. Raising standards of attainment and of behaviour may have some slight effect on who is regarded as having special needs, but none on how many pupils are regarded as falling into this category. The reason, as indicated earlier in the chapter, is that the decision to regard 20 per cent of pupils as having special needs at some stage in their school careers is essentially both an arbitrary and a political one. It cannot in any meaningful way be said to be based on research, though the way tests and behaviour screening instruments are constructed ensures that 'research' will always be available to justify it.

The fact remains, though, that schools vary widely in the number of pupils they appear to regard as having special needs. This does *not* imply that some schools have no pupils with special needs. Galloway (1983), Rutter *et al.* (1979) and Reynolds (1976) have all described characteristics of successful schools. The success of these schools may well disguise the existence of pupils who would be regarded as problems in other schools. Meeting special needs effectively removes pupils from the lime-light.

At other schools pupils and teachers seem to be locked into a vicious cycle. Low morale amongst teachers reflects, and is reflected in, disaffected behaviour and low educational attainments in the pupils. The schools' responses to pupils' behaviour and learning difficulties can unfortunately generate further disaffection in the pupils, leading to still lower teacher morale.

In Chapters 4 – 8 we describe how some schools may successfully meet pupils's special needs, while others aggravate existing needs and generate new ones. First, though, we must consider the administrative and legal implications for schools as conceived in the 1981 Eduction Act and take a closer look at the vexed question of the assessment of the children concerned. In the process we will analyse some of the underlying assumptions of the new legislation, and explore some of the inconsistencies in its concept of special needs.

2 ADMINISTRATIVE AND LEGAL ISSUES

Introduction

The 1981 Education Act was the government's response to the Warnock Report. It was clear from the outset that the report itself would constitute a landmark in the education of children with special needs. Since one of the report's central conclusions was that most such children were, and would remain, in ordinary schools, there was a general expectation that its influence would be felt throughout ordinary and special schools well into the twenty-first century.

At first sight the 1981 Education Act appears to introduce far-reaching changes with major implications for teachers both in ordinary and in special schools, and for members of the support services. A closer look is less reassuring. This chapter summarises the background to the Act and the Act itself. It then analyses some inconsistencies in the Act and discusses possible implications for l.e.a. support services and for teachers in ordinary schools. We conclude that while the Act undoubtedly has implications for ordinary schools, there are no grounds for optimism about its likely impact.

Background to the 1981 Education Act

Prior to the 1981 Act the legislative basis for special education lay in the 1944 Education Act. Children could be 'ascertained' by a school medical officer as suffering from a 'disability of mind or body'. The Ministry of Education (1959) laid down ten categories of handicap. Broadly, these dealt with physical and sensory handicaps but included 'educationally sub-normal' and 'maladjusted' pupils.

Responsibility for ascertainment lay with school medical officers for two reasons. First, handicap was seen primarily as a medical problem, and few doctors or educationists had started seriously to question the *non sequitur* that special medical problems required special educational help. It was inconvenient that no consistent medical criteria were at hand to 'diagnose' subnormality or malad-justment, but psychologists helped out by training school doctors to administer the Stanford Binet Intelligence Scale, a popular intelligence test for individual administration. The second reason for the medical control over entry to special education following the 1944 Act was that doctors were the only specialists available in sufficient numbers, educational psychology still being in its infancy as a profession.

Not surprisingly, changes in educational thinking led to ques-tions both about the ideas behind special education in the 1944 Act and about their implementation in practice. An issue which was contentious almost from the start was the degree of formality re-quired in the proceedings. The 1944 Education Act made clear that formal ascertainment was not necessary for a child to be admitted to a special school. Many l.e.a.'s, however, insisted on formally ascertaining all children placed in special schools as suffering from one of the ten categories of handicap. This served to emphasise the separate nature of special education, with an implicit assumption that 'special' education could only be provided in schools or classes recognised by the DES as efficient for the education of children with a particular category of handicap. The formality helped to ensure that tranfer from special schools to the mainstream was a rare event.

A second issue that gradually became increasingly contentious throughout the 1950s and 1960s was the medical responsibility for ascertainment. Children were being referred to special schools for educational problems, but on medical criteria. As early as 1958 the Ministry of Education's chief Medical Officer recommended that head teachers and educational psychologists should contribute to placement decisions. Thus, a consensus gradually emerged that special education should be seen essentially as an educational matter, though medical advice would clearly continue to be needed on the likely implications of medical factors for a child's educa-tional needs.

With the emphasis on educational needs came recognition that the distinction between 'special' and 'ordinary' children was to a large extent arbitrary. The criteria for admission to special schools depended on the availability of places. Decisions were often made on the basis of test scores. It was known that intelligence test scores could vary by at least 15 IQ points on two occasions in a short space of time, and similar problems existed with attainment tests. More seriously still, there was growing recognition that a child's performance could be affected not only by family background but also by the quality of teaching at school.

Recognition that the distinction between 'ordinary' and 'special' children was not clear-cut carried an obvious implication for the ten categories of handicap. If special need was to be defined in educational terms, and if no hard and fast cut-off points existed, then clearly the categories had outlived their usefulness. Related to this, the overlap between categories was so large as to render them valueless in practice. To take a not altogether unusual example, 10-year-old Derek with an IQ of 70 and a reading age of 7 could have been considered ESN(M). The fact that Derek also had a significant hearing loss, suffered from epilepsy, had been confined to a wheel chair since a road accident, and that adults found his behaviour extremely disturbing could have enabled him to qualify for four more of the original ten categories.

Recognition of all these issues came in a circular from the DES (1975) which advised that formal medical examinations as laid down in the 1944 Act should be used only in the very rare instances where a l.e.a. wished to enforce special school attendance against a parent's wishes. The circular emphasised the importance of medical examinations, but urged that they should be carried out before the child was seen by an educational psychologist, and that formal ascertainment should generally be regarded as unnecessary. A corollary of this was that transfer in and out of special schools could, in principal, be a great deal more flexible. It was hoped that this would help to break down the barriers between special and mainstream schools, and help to emphasise the role of the latter in meeting special needs.

Two further trends in educational thought must be mentioned. These are the international movement in favour of integration, or mainstreaming in American parlance, and directly related demands from parents that they should have greater influence on how and where their children should be educated. The case for integrating children with physical or sensory disabilities into the mainstream has been discussed elsewhere (e.g. Anderson, 1973; Cope and Anderson, 1977; Hegarty and Pocklington, 1982, 1983).

Perhaps a more important point here is that the debate on integration concentrated mainly on the needs of children with physical and sensory disabilities. Relatively little attention was paid to the numerically much larger groups of ESN(M) and maladjusted pupils. The probable reason is that these groups, unlike most of the other categories recognised under the 1944 Act, lacked the support of local, well-organised parent pressure groups. A further point is that pressure to remove these children arose because of their supposed failure or inability to conform to the demands of ordinary classes. In contrast, it could be argued that children with physical and sensory disabilities had been referred to special schools in spite of, and not because of, their ability to cope, with appropriate help, in the mainstream (Galloway and Goodwin, 1979).

The Warnock Report did not explore this point in detail. The Committee did, however, acknowledge the case for integrating children with special needs into ordinary schools, though with certain caveats to which we shall return. More important, they also acknowledged the case for forging closer links between teachers in special schools and ordinary schools, so that meeting special educational needs would eventually be seen as a routine requirement in ordinary schools. The explicit emphasis on the special needs of up to 20 per cent of pupils, rather than the 2 per cent hitherto placed in special schools reflected the committee's view that special and mainstream education must not be rigidly divided. The recommendation to abolish the categories of handicap, replacing them with the broader concept of special educational need reflected the logical and administrative anomalies arising from the former system. Emphasis on parental involvement in decision-making and on the importance of multi-professional assessment can also be seen as reflecting an emerging consensus on what constituted good practice.

The 1981 Education Act

The Act provides an entirely new legislative framework for meeting special needs. At least in theory, it contains as many implications for teachers in ordinary schools as for the traditional special school and special class network. The former categories of handicap are replaced by a generic concept of learning difficulty, including physical and intellectual disabilities. Any child with a learning difficulty requiring educational provision which differs from or is additional to the provision generally made for children of the same age in an ordinary school is said to have special educational needs.

For the first time in educational law in Britain, the Act

acknowledges the principle of integration. (Section 10 of the 1976 Education Act also acknowledged this principle, but was superseded by the 1981 Education Act before Section 10 was implemented). Children with special educational needs should, according to the Act, be educated in an ordinary school subject to:

(1) Parental wishes.
(2) The possibility of meeting the individual child's needs in an ordinary school.
(3) 'Provision of efficient education for the children with whom he will be educated'.
(4) 'The efficient use of resources'.

The Act requires l.e.a.'s to identify children with special needs. It also places an explicit responsibility on the governors of maintained and voluntary schools 'to use their best endeavours' to ensure that a child's special needs are made known to all his teachers and that the required special provision is provided. In practice the headteacher is responsible to the governors or managers for ensuring that special needs are recognised and met.

The Act places a further duty on teachers in ordinary schools, and hence on the school's governors. Teachers of any child with special needs attending an ordinary school shall ensure, as far as is 'reasonably practicable, that the child engages in the activities of the school together with children who do not have special educational needs'. Full-time segregation from ordinary pupils, while paying lip-service to the idea of integration, is thus officially discouraged. The main proviso is that enabling the child to engage in the activities of the school should not be incompatible with the efficient use of resources or the provision of efficient education for other children in the school.

The Act introduces elaborate machinery for parental involvement in identifying their children's needs and deciding how they should be met. The DES has frequently paid lip service to the notion of consultation and co-operation with parents. In the 1981 Act, for the first time in special education law, this becomes mandatory. Parents are entitled to request that their child's needs be assessed. If the l.e.a. decides, after preliminary inquiries, not to carry out a full assessment, the parents have a right of appeal to the Secretary of State. They also have a right of comment if the l.e.a. decides to assess their child's needs following a request from a teacher, doctor or member of the education support services.

The Act lays down in considerable detail the advice the l.e.a. must obtain when determining a child's special educational needs. As a minimum, the authority must seek advice from the child's teachers, from a school medical officer and from an educational psychologist. In addition, advice may be sought from other professionals such as social workers or child psychiatrists. Parents must be notifed of the dates and times of each assessment, and in general have the right to be present. The exceptions are that they have no right to attend 'assessment over a period of time in the classroom or other setting', and that 'some forms of psychological testing may need to be carried out without the presence of observers, including parents'.

Having carried out a full assessment, the l.e.a. may decide not to issue a 'Statement' determining the special educational provision that should be made for the child. This clause covers instances in which the l.e.a. feels that no special provision is required. If parents disagree, however, they may appeal to the Secretary of State.

If the l.e.a. does decide to issue a Statement, a draft must be sent to parents, who have the right to make representations. These include meeting an officer of the l.e.a., and further meetings to discuss professional advice which the authority has received. The authority must include copies of the reports it has received in the course of the assessment with the draft statement. This is the first time parents have been given the right to see professional reports on which decisions about special education are based. After considering the parents' view, the authority can decide to amend the Statement, or to issue it in its original form. If they still disagree with the Statement, parents can appeal to a local Appeals Committee which can confirm the Statement or ask the l.e.a. to reconsider it. As a last resort, parents have the right of appeal to the Secretary of State for Education and Science.

It is clear from this summary that parents' rights are spelled out in minute detail. The examinations on which professionals base their assessment are not spelled out in similar detail. In view of continual changes and developments in professional practice this would almost certainly be impracticable. Fifteen years ago, for example, most educational psychologists would have regarded an intelligence test as an essential part of their assessment. There is no longer general agreement on this. The DES (1983) has nevertheless provided advice in the form of a suggested checklist for professionals to consider while carrying out their assessments. The checklist contains three broad headings:

(1) Description of the child's functioning.
(2) The aims of special educational provision.
(3) The facilities and resources necessary to provide it.

We return to these when considering assessment in more detail in Chapter 3.

The 1981 Act's emphasis on parental rights is consistent with the emphasis on parents as partners with teachers in their children's education, advocated in the Warnock Report. In turn, the report reflected the growing influence of well-organised associations of parents of children with particular disabilities. Parental pressure for integration has seldom been welcomed by teachers in special schools or in ordinary schools. On the other hand it could be uncharitable to imply that they have generally resisted parents' efforts to co-operate in their children's educational programmes. Co-operation has, however, been more widespread in schools for children with physical and sensory disabilities and severe intellectual handicaps, than in schools for children with moderate learning difficulties or for children with behavioural or emotional problems.

The Act's insistence on parental rights can also be seen in a wider context. The previous year, the 1980 Education Act had greatly increased parents' rights to choose their children's school. This Act also obliged schools to make more information available to parents than had previously been required, including information on examination results in secondary schools. With some reservations, discussed below, the 1981 Act may be seen as an attempt to extend parental rights in the special education field, as the 1980 Act had with respect to ordinary schools.

Some Anomalies in the 1981 Education Act

The Concept of Need

It would be odd if the Act did not confine itself to consideration of children's special needs. Acts of Parliament are not the usual place to discuss controversial professional issues such as the school's influence on whether children can be said to have special needs. Yet the concept of need implicit in the Act is not at all straightforward.

When we talk about someone having a need for something we are making a disguised value judgement. We may mean that we think he ought to have the thing in question. Alternatively, we may mean the person thinks he ought to have it. In either case the statement implies some conception of the person's welfare. Simply wanting something carries no implication of needing it. If we say we need something, we are probably saying that we want it, but not necessarily. Definitely, however, we are implying that we would benefit in some way from the thing in question.

Children do not, on the whole, say that they have special educational needs. Teachers and/or parents make this claim. In doing so they are implying a value judgement about the help which they believe the child ought to be receiving. Less obviously, they may also be implying a value judgement about the progress the child ought to be making. This is essentially a pragmatic argument. A blind child who is agreed by all concerned to be making excellent progress still has special educational needs. In the case of a slow-learning child this may also be the case. More frequently, however, the child is said to have special needs because he is not thought to be making adequate progress. In the case of children presenting behavioural problems, ascribing special needs can be seen still more clearly to result from the teacher's feeling that the child ought to be behaving differently. Everyone concerned may agree that the child is making excellent progress in view of his background and/or constitutional problems. Yet as long as he is thought to have continuing special needs there is an implication that further change is desirable.

It follows, then, that in saying a child has special educational needs teachers are also implying something about what they themselves want. They may say, with complete sincerity, that they want the best for the child. They may also say, with equal sincerity that their first concern is the welfare of other children in the class, whose progress is suffering from the presence of a child with special needs. Both statements describe what the teacher wants. Unfortunately the two 'wants' are not always compatible.

Most educational psychologists can recall without difficulty occasions when remaining in the mainstream would have been in the child's best interests. In a seminal article, Dunn (1968) remarked that if he had known: 'what I now know about special classes for the educable mentally retarded, other things being equal I would then go to court before allowing the schools to label my child as "mentally retarded" and place him in a "self-contained special school or class" '. The continuing controversy over admission of pupils to ESN(M) schools, special schools for the maladjusted and off-site centres for disruptive pupils in this country raises similar questions about what is in the child's best interests.

The point, developed in the next chapter, is that children are frequently considered to have special needs when their teachers find their behaviour or progress disturbing. This implies no critical value judgement on the teachers' competence, nor on their priorities. Teachers are fully justified in arguing that their first concern must be the progress and well-being of the majority. Nevertheless, confusing what children need with what teachers want is not without danger.

The problem is illustrated by considering one of the research projects mentioned in Chapter 1. Galloway *et al.* (1982a) described huge differences between secondary schools in the number of pupils they suspended. These differences could not be attributed to differences in the schools' catchment area (Galloway *et al.*, 1984a). In practical terms this meant that over a four-year period one Sheffield school produced more than 50 pupils who could be said to have special needs on the grounds that their behaviour had led to suspension from school. In the same period another school, with twice as many pupils and serving at least as disadvantaged a catchment area, produced none. The differences in suspension rates were reflected both in the behaviour of pupils in the schools concerned and in the attitudes of teachers. There would seem to have been a need for change in the school with a high suspension rate. In other words, the school's teachers had needs which were just as pressing as those of their disruptive pupils.

The last statement clearly implies a value judgement about the school concerned. To say that the pupils who were suspended had special educational needs would perhaps have been reasonable. Many of them certainly wanted a change of school, and it could be argued that their lack of progress and disruptive behaviour indicated their need for a change. Just as certainly, their teachers wanted them to be moved. Yet describing these pupils' special educational needs without reference to the needs of their teachers would, at best, have been dishonest. The implication would have been that the problem concerned the pupils alone. In fact, the pupils could reasonably be seen as the product of their schools.

The DES (1983) seems to side-step the issues of teachers' needs in its advice on assessment. The suggested checklist of areas for consideration includes such topics as cognitive and social development, and the emotional climate and social regime which the child needs. The focus, though, remains clearly on the child. In no way can the assessment be said to include full consideration of the needs of teachers, as reflected in the pupils they refer to the l.e.a. as having special educational needs.

Integration

The Act purports to support the general idea of integrating children with special needs in ordinary schools. It may well succeed in this aim with respect to children with physical and sensory disabilities. In terms of children with moderate learning difficulties and behavioural or emotional problems, formerly classsified as ESN(M) and maladjusted, the Act's influence will almost certainly be very limited. To see why, it is worth considering developments over the last few years in one l.e.a.

Goodwin (1983) describes the education support services in Sheffield, a city with a long tradition of commitment to special education. In 1976 the education committee formally adopted a policy of integration, and in 1977 set up a 'support teacher' service in which teachers experienced in special education were appointed to offer guidance and help to colleagues teaching children with special needs in ordinary schools. Starting with 7 teachers, by 1981, the number had increased to 22. The support teachers were attached to centres for children with mild learning difficulties, and schools for the maladjusted, physically handicapped and ESN(M). These teachers were appointed in addition to peripatetic teachers for children with visual or hearing impairments, and to the l.e.a.'s existing psychological service. Their appointment was welcomed by teachers in ordinary schools.

As the support services are naturally expected to implement the city council's integration policy, one way to evaluate their activities is in terms of the number of pupils admitted to separate special schools. It is worth repeating here that the support teacher service was based on the notion of helping teachers to meet special educational needs in the ordinary school system. Further, most of the l.e.a.'s educational psychologists supported the general idea of integration.

In 1976 – 7, 226 Sheffield pupils were placed in special schools, with a slight increase the following two years to 237 and 264. By

1979 – 80 the number had increased to 346, a peak which was maintained the following year. In the same period 1976 – 81, the total school population in Sheffield fell by nearly 13 per cent. Goodwin (1982) comments:

> Thus over this five-year period, when the policy from Sheffield education committee was to proceed with the integration of the handicapped, more children were placed into special schools, and the percentage of children within them continued to grow . . . All of the professionals involved may well be doing other things, but they are certainly not keeping children within the ordinary schools who would otherwise be going out into the special school system. (p. 164)

We explore in Chapter 3 some of the reasons for the apparent impotence of the education support services to pursue a policy to which their employer is committed and which they as individuals support. The question here is: will the 1981 Education Act make any difference? Two major aspects of the Act are relevant here. The first is the Act's commitment, in theory, to integration. The second is the rights it gives parents in deciding how their children's educational needs should be met.

The Act's commitment to integration can be dismissed quickly. Only two of the 'escape clauses' need to be repeated: children with special needs should be educated in ordinary schools, subject to 'provision of efficient education' for the other children in the school, and 'the efficient use of resources'. The point is that these two clauses could have been, and in many cases undoubtedly were, invoked to justify the transfer out of ordinary schools of *all* pupils currently attending separate special schools for the ESN(M) and the maladjusted. Brief consideration of each clause will illustrate this argument.

We have already argued that children are referred because their teachers find them disturbing. It implies neither malice nor insincerity on the part of ordinary school teachers to note that their concern about children with learning and behavioural problems may be motivated as much by these children's effect on other pupils as by the needs of the pupils themselves. With a class of up to 35, there is an obvious limit to the time and attention a teacher can justify spending on one or two individuals.

The 1981 Act requires l.e.a.'s to obtain approval from the

Secretary of State before closing special schools. Efficient use of resources requires that existing schools should be used. In Sheffield the l.e.a. has in the past expressed a commitment to special education by opening separate special schools, (and has in fact continued to open new special schools since introducing its integration policy). A similar situation exists in many other l.e.a.'s. The existing special schools constitute an obvious resource, which — just as obviously — must be used unless there is irrefutable evidence that the need no longer exists.

Warnock's definition of special needs ensures that this evidence will never be provided. With 20 per cent of pupils regarded as having special needs at some stage in their school career, it becomes quite ludicrous to expect that schools will cheerfully retain the two per cent of children, or fewer, who had hitherto been placed in separate special schools. The number of places in special schools for the ESN(M) and maladjusted has increased enormously since 1944. Special school places have been supplemented by part-time centres for children with learning difficulties and by off-site units for disruptive pupils who seldom return to the mainstream. Yet the demand for places continues to exceed supply, in spite of the evidence, reviewed in Chapter 1, that teachers in the 1920s and 1930s were concerned about as many children as their successors in the 1980s.

The explanation lies partly in the variety of Parkinson's Law which states that the number of pupils with learning or behavioural problems thought to need separate special educational help will continually increase to exceed the available supply. This appears less cynical against the background of an extended definition of special needs as advocated by Warnock and by the 1981 Education Act. There is no doubt, though, that separate special schools can be self-maintaining, nor that they act to prevent their pupils' integration into the mainstream. An excellent example of the way their existence can be destructive to an integration policy is given by Booth (1983).

The integration of children with severe learning difficulties into infant schools in Bromley had aroused national recognition and praise, benefitting both the intellectually handicapped children and the 'ordinary' pupils. At the same time that the authority was starting to integrate intellectually handicapped children into ordinary schools, it was obtaining approval for a new ESN(S) school. Unfortunately the demand for places was over-estimated. As a result, the new school was designed for 100 pupils, but opened with only 12. Booth comments:

> Once it had been built the new special school created pressures of its own. Its existence had to be justified. The only infant and junior school to have groups of mentally handicapped children had one group who were profoundly handicapped. This group moved across to the new special school to make the numbers more respectable and gradually its numbers built up to a reasonable level. While he (the former assistant education officer for Bromley) recognised that the new school was good as a special school, he did think that a mistake had been made. (p. 49)

Parents Rights

There is no reason for thinking that the statutory rights granted to parents in the 1981 Act will have any effect on the number of children transferred out of ordinary schools to separate special schools on account of learning difficulties and/or behaviour problems. The reasons are very simple. Again, they are illustrated by policy and practice in Sheffield.

In 1975 a DES Circular advocated informality in transferring pupils to special schools; formal ascertainment, as we have seen, was recommended only in extreme cases where the l.e.a. wished to enforce attendances against parents' wishes. At least in Sheffield, this occurred seldom, if ever. Probably all the children admitted to special schools in 1976–81 were admitted with their parents' consent. Commendably, l.e.a. policy encouraged parents to visit possible special schools before making a final decision that they wanted their child to transfer. While parents were not generally given copies of professional reports, educational psychologists expected as a matter of course to discuss the child's needs with parents, and were most unlikely to recommend special school transfer unless they were satisfied that the parents agreed with the recommendation.

Parents may not always have been altogether happy about their child's transfer. Indeed agreement may have been based less on a feeling that special schools offered something special than that ordinary schools had rejected their child. Yet there was no instance in which the l.e.a. sought to enforce attendance against a parent's explicit wish. The position in Sheffield was not atypical. Although conflict could and did occur from time to time, at no stage since 1944 was the DES, or its predecessor the Ministry of Education, overwhelmed by appeals from parents objecting to the l.e.a.'s attempt to enforce attendance at a special school. It is really very difficult to see what will change as a result of the 1981 Act.

Formality of the Procedures

From 1944 – 81 formal ascertainment was required, in theory, only when the l.e.a. wished to enforce attendance at a special school against parents' wishes. The 1975 DES Circular effectively halted formal ascertainment by school medical officers. The emphasis was on consultation between professionals, and between professionals and parents. It was hoped that special schools would increasingly be used flexibly, with minimal formality in admission and discharge procedures. In this way, the barriers between special and mainstream schools would be broken down, leading to greater mutual understanding and respect. The 1981 Act has no such pretensions.

All admissions to a separate special school for a prolonged period must now be based on a formal Statement of the children's special educational needs, indicating the form of special provision they require (DES, 1983). Children can, it is true, be admitted on a temporary basis in emergencies, but the period of admission must be specified and in practice must be no longer than the time needed to prepare a Statement. Transfer from a special school to the mainstream requires a full re-assessment. Further, parents are not permitted to withdraw their children from special schools without the l.e.a.'s permission. Newell (1983) points out that this is discriminatory, as the ruling does not apply to children in ordinary schools.

It is fairly clear, therefore, that what the DES (1983) euphemistically refers to as the 'protection' of a Statement may in fact constitute a funnel into special schools. Parents do not always recognise the high probability that referral to a separate special school will be 'terminal', implying that the child will remain in special education until he reaches school leaving age. Prior to the 1981 Act, parents could simply withdraw their child from a special school. Except in the very few cases when the child had been formally ascertained, the l.e.a. would then have to decide whether to ascertain the child, in order to enforce attendance, or to permit transfer to a mainstream school. In most cases their inclination would be towards the latter option, perhaps with the stipulation that admission was initially for a trial period.

The formality of the assessment process in the 1981 Act may well lead to greater caution in recommending, in the formal Statement, that a child's needs should be met in an ordinary school. This is partly because head-teachers and school governors may oppose retaining pupils with special needs unless the l.e.a. is willing to provide extra resources. For pupils already attending special schools, many professionals may doubt whether the curriculum and regime constitute a suitable preparation for return to the mainstream. The length and complexity of re-assessment procedures may act as a further disincentive to exploring the possibility of return to the mainstream. This remains a matter for research. It is clear, however, that the 1981 Act has replaced the possibility of flexible, informal transfer in and out of special schools with the certainty of a lengthy, complex and highly bureaucratic process. We have argued that this will not substantially reduce admissions to special schools. It may well make discharge more difficult.

Implications for Ordinary Schools

The 1981 Act has important implications for policy and practice in ordinary schools. How much impact it will have is open to debate. So far we have suggested that its impact may be much less than is widely supposed. Welton *et al.* (1982) make two important observations in this connection:

> Fundamental change is unlikely to occur without simultaneous developments in the administrative structure, in relationships between professionals, administrators and users, and without changes in practice, attitudes and ideas. We have found in our research that the most specific aspects of the SE[1] procedures instituted following Circular 2/75[2] were not generally implemented as intended, but either became adapted to local use or ritualised as a *post hoc* means of recording or justifying decision making. (p. 48)

---

(1) Special Education
(2) DES, 1975

There is little doubt that the procedures set out in the 1981 Act are just as open to 'adaptation' and subversion as the proposals of 1975. The Act contains nothing to ensure fundamental changes in special education practice. Like much education law, the Act reflects a rather broad consensus on what constitutes good practice. Its proposals for integration are much weaker than those of comparable laws in other countries, such as the United States (1975). *Education for All Handicapped Children Act.* All head teachers of ordinary schools can rest assured that the Act requires little fundamental change in their policy or practices. The only innovations which they cannot evade can safely be regarded as peripheral, provided they are handled with a modicum of care and tact. The Act does nevertheless hold important implications for ordinary schools, even though most of these implications can safely be ignored by those so inclined. The rest of this chapter identifies the most far-reaching implications, discusses how some schools will certainly evade them, and suggests that others will respond more constructively.

Extending the Concept of Special Educational Needs

We have argued already that the Act will probably not result in any decline in the number of pupils referred to separate special schools. The extended concept of special needs should nevertheless ensure that schools review their provision for the least able and most disturbing 20 per cent of their pupils. In many schools these pupils have in the past been grouped under all-embracing amorphous categories of 'remedial' and 'disruptive'. The Warnock Report's insistence that both groups had special educational needs was strengthened by its penetrating critique of the concept of remedial education:

At present 'remedial' groups include children with a variety of difficulties which, though different in origin, are frequently treated alike . . . the term 'remedial', like the term 'treatment', suggests that these children have something wrong with them that can be put right. It is true that some of them are suffering only a temporary learning difficulty and, given appropriate help, are able to return rapidly to their previous classes having completely overcome their disability. Others, however, require special help and support throughout their school lives and to say that these children require 'remedial' education is misleading. Children in these so-called 'remedial' groups have a wide variety of individual needs, sometimes linked to psychological or physical factors, which call for skilled and discriminating attention by staff — in assessment, the devising of suitable programmes and the organisation of group or individual teaching, whether in ordinary or special classes. (DES, 1978*a*, p. 47)

The question, though, is whether the 1981 Act will in fact lead to more discriminating attention to these pupils. The obstacles are formidable. The government has made no extra money available to schools. At a time of economic pressure, compounded by pressures associated with falling rolls, finding extra resources becomes well nigh impossible. The jobs of part-time teachers, formerly responsible for 'remedial' groups in ordinary schools become an irresistible target for cost-conscious administrators. Head teachers are able to say: 'We recognise Timmy's special needs. We would love to be able to meet them, but without extra resources we are unable to do so. We must therefore request that he be transferred to a school better able to cater for his special needs'.

The l.e.a. can reply that the school ought to be able to cater adequately for the child, and issue a Statement to this effect, following a formal assessment. Provided the parents agree, the school will then be required to try to meet Timmy's needs as specified in the Statement. Further, they will have to co-operate in annual reviews.

The practice, however, is not quite so straightforward. Unless there is strong pressure from parents, a l.e.a. may be reluctant to recommend that a child remains in an ordinary school in which teachers have said quite explicitly that they feel unable to meet his needs. As every educational psychologist knows, insisting that a child should remain in a school which wants his removal is a recipe for disaster. The child's continuing educational and behavioural problems can subsequently be taken as vindication of the school's original assessment that nothing useful could be done without extra resources.

Parents' Rights

Together, the 1980 and 1981 Education Acts have far-reaching implications for the relationship between ordinary school teachers and their pupils' parents. As a result of the 1981 Act head teachers will have to consult parents before requesting a formal assessment of their child. In addition, their reports, which form part of the assessment, will be available to parents. This may not change existing practice very much. In many l.e.a.'s, educational psychologists have for years refused to accept referrals without parental agreement. In effect, the Act merely stipulates minimum acceptable standards. Nothing can ensure that an Act is observed in spirit as well as to the letter. In practice communication with parents can range from provision of information that the child's progress and/or behaviour are unsatisfactory, to an active partnership in which parents are seen as contributing with teachers in identifying and meeting their children's special needs.

The unknown factor is how many parents will formally apply to the l.e.a. for an assessment. The l.e.a. 'cannot unreasonably refuse' to consider a request, and in practice is unlikely to refuse to carry out a formal assessment of the child's needs if the parents insist. Yet unless parents request assessment, the DES (1983) makes clear that formal assessment should only be necessary when the child's needs are thought 'to require provision additional to or otherwise different from, the facilities and resources generally available in ordinary schools'. Hence, without parental requests, an ordinary school may contain no pupils with the 'protection' of a Statement determining the special educational provision they require.

The 'protection' of a Statement may not be as impressive as it appears in theory. Following assessment the l.e.a. can suggest in the draft Statement that the child be transferred to a separate special school. This could be a way to avoid providing additional resources in the child's ordinary school. If the parents object, the l.e.a. could offer to withdraw the Statement, in which case the child will remain in the ordinary school, or decide to issue it unaltered. The latter course leaves the parent the opportunity to appeal to the local Appeals Committee and ultimately to the Secretary of State. If the appeal fails, though, the l.e.a. will be able to enforce attendance at a special school against the parents' wishes.

Governors and the Local Education Authority

Governors can handle their responsibilities under the Act in different ways. They can take an active interest, seeing the head as accountable to them for the school's policy towards children with special needs and for the implementation of this policy in practice.

Alternatively they can take a passive interest, relying on the head to tell them as much, or as little, as they need to know. For their part, head teachers can use a variety of tactics to stimulate, or inhibit, the governors' interest.

A somewhat similar situation exists with respect to the school's relationship with the l.e.a. Under the new Act l.e.a.'s have a duty to arrange special educational provision in accordance with the formal Statement on the child's needs. They will presumably be reluctant to recommend ordinary school placement in the Statement if:

(1) the school is unwilling, *or*
(2) extra expense would by incurred.

The l.e.a. is in a position, though, actively to promote an integration policy through its advisers, educational psychologists and other support services. The l.e.a. can stimulate interest in ways of catering for children with special needs, and can publicise examples of successful practice. Some l.e.a. policies and practices promoting special education provision in ordinary schools are discussed in Chapters 4 and 5. We must also note, however, that the l.e.a. can also adopt a much more passive role. In this case, the l.e.a. responds to requests from parents or teachers, meeting all the requirements imposed by the Act while doing little or nothing to promote a coherent and co-ordinated policy throughout its schools.

Conclusions

This chapter has suggested that the 1981 Act will not necessarily change existing practice to the extent expected by the DES and by the professionals advising the government. The Act can legitimately be criticised for failing to give stronger encouragement to a policy of integration, and for failing to make resources available to assist ordinary schools in meeting their pupils' special needs. On the other hand, the function of educational law in this country has generally been to encourage good practice without stipulating in detail precisely how it should be carried out. The Act is not a charter for parents of children with special needs. Its benefits to parents and children may not be as great as its sponsors hoped. Yet here too we must again distinguish between the Act's implications and its possible impact. Its impact can undoubtedly be greatly reduced if local administrators and teachers, within ordinary and special schools, lack the will or the vision to implement it in the spirit as well as conforming to its bureaucratic details. The Act nevertheless provides a framework which could lead to far-reaching changes. In the next chapter we consider implications for assessment procedures in ordinary schools.

3 ASSESSMENT

Introduction

Assessment is not a once-and-for-all procedure, but rather a continuing process, forming an integral part of teaching throughout the school. Effective teaching implies continual assessment of children's progress and of their understanding. This applies as much to pupils of average and above average ability as to pupils with special needs. Outside the statutory framework created by the 1981 Education Act, there is no logical reason to regard the assessment of these pupils as raising separate issues of principle to those affecting the majority who are not regarded as having special needs. Assessment, then, must be seen as part of a school's policy and practice towards all its pupils, and not as a discrete set of procedures for identifying special needs.

In theory the broad aim of assessment is straightforward: to monitor children's progress, and hence to determine how teachers may best meet their needs. Within the same class children will have widely differing experiences, attainment and ability. Effective teaching is not possible without some understanding of such differences. Yet as so often happens, the purposes of assessment become more problematic on closer inspection. This chapter discusses some stated and unstated aims of assessment. Next we consider the levels at which assessment can take place, with particular reference to children with special needs. Finally we consider some possible implications for policy and practice throughout the school.

A Starting Point

Children are influenced by, and influence, the people around them. At its most simple level, this can be seen in any classroom. The teacher creates, or fails to create an ordered atmosphere conducive to learning. Depending on their teacher's skill and commitment, children make varying amounts of progress. Controlling for social class, the differences over a year between the progress of pupils in different classes within a primary school are greater than the differences between schools (Bennett, 1976). In other words, children's progress over a year depends at least as much, and probably more, on their class-teacher as on which school they happen to be attending.

Yet pupils also affect the teacher's attitude and behaviour. Teachers often talk of having 'an exceptionally difficult class this year', or of a class being 'totally different when two particular kids are away ill'. In such cases teachers are referring implicitly to the effect which a particular class or a particular individual have on them. How teachers react varies from individual to individual. Some try to 'clamp down' on the class as a whole, or on one or two troublesome pupils. Others try consciously to reduce tension by demanding less in terms of work or behaviour. Finding new ways to introduce the syllabus, and 'counselling' particular pupils are further possibilities. The point is that neither the pupils' nor the teacher's behaviour can be seen in isolation, but rather as a product of the interaction between them.

Even this, however, is an over-simplification. The teacher's classroom behaviour will certainly be affected both by school policy and by staff room ethos. There are schools in which senior staff oppose 'progressive' ideas, regaling anyone who will listen with accounts of the chaos following the introduction of 'new fangled' methods by enthusiastic probationers fresh from college. A newly appointed member of staff at such a school will quickly be socialised into accepting the group's norm. Even if he is not privately convinced, he will need great strength of character to risk ridicule from older, more experienced colleagues. The reverse also applies. Innovation is possible in a climate in which senior staff encourage new ideas, regarding failure not as a sign of the innovator's personal or professional inadequacy but as a potentially useful learning experience.

Children's behaviour and progress, too, is not simply influenced by what happens in the classroom. Adverse family circumstances, including excessive academic pressure from home, can exert an important influence. The same applies to wider factors within the school. Primary children coming to the classroom straight from an energetic PE session, ending on a high note with no opportunity to 'unwind', may take a long time to settle. In secondary schools, it is not uncommon for teachers to find pupils restless, unsettled and badly behaved when they have just had a double session with a particularly tough disciplinarian immediately beforehand.

Seen in this light, assessment of individual needs cannot be divorced from the wider social context. Unfortunately, assessment usually focuses on the individual, ignoring other influences. Nowhere is this more of a problem than in assessment of children with special needs. Too frequently, assessment concentrates on the child and the child's family, to the exclusion of school and classroom factors. These may have a more direct bearing on his educational needs than family factors. Moreover, teachers have greater control over the school and classroom than over the child's background.

The argument that children affect, and are affected by, their surroundings has some far-reaching implications for the concept of assessment. It implies that:

(1) Traditional techniques using published tests and checklists can be seen, at best, only as part of an assessment.
(2) An attempt must be made to integrate information about the child, information from parents, and information relating to the school in general and the classroom in particular.
(3) Assessment of individual pupils and evaluation of teachers and of the school as an institution are not separate activities, but must be seen as inter-related.

The Purpose of Assessment

We have already seen how special schools can create their own demand for children to fill them (Booth, 1983). Neither the policy of the l.e.a.'s Education Committee nor the preferences of most of the l.e.a.'s educational psychologists nor the appointment of support teachers to help teachers in ordinary schools cater for pupils with special needs appear able to withstand this demand (Goodwin, 1983). The fact that formal ascertainment was seldom used to enforce attendence at special school prior to the 1981 Act did not necessarily imply active parental consent. Parents acquiesced, but evidence suggests that some did so with reluctance (e.g. Beresford *et al.*, 1983). In some cases placement was the source of bitter and lasting resentment (e.g. Coard, 1971), even though there is no evidence that, in theory, it was enforced against parents' wishes.

There is a direct parallel within ordinary schools. Just as some pupils are transferred out of ordinary schools 'for their own good', and nominally with parental consent, so others are identified for special treatment in their own schools. The special treatment can go by a variety of names: the remedial department, the C Band, even the 'community service class'. Parents are not always informed, let alone consulted when their child is selected for some 'special' help. When they are consulted, or when they themselves raise objections the usual reply is that the child can't cope with the demands of the more academic class, which may be working towards external examinations, and will benefit from a curriculum more suited to his needs.

Pupils, however, are seldom convinced. Hargreaves (1983) describes the reactions of pupils in an examination form and in a community service group. Both pupils make quite clear that the true function of the community service group is to facilitate the progress of the 'academic' pupils, enabling teachers to spend more time with them while the remainder do something practical which keeps them out of the way. In this connection, it is not coincidence that a disproportionate number of new curriculum initiatives has focused on the curriculum for less able pupils. The reason is clearly that innovations which are possible with non-examination pupils would meet resistance from parents and employers and — most important of all — examination boards if extended to include the academically most able 20 per cent.

At one level it makes little difference whether the school has mixed ability classes, streams pupils according to ability, or divides them into two or three ability 'bands' with classes of mixed ability within each band. In his early work Hargreaves (1967) thought that streaming facilitated the development of an anti-school subculture in older secondary school pupils. Other work, however, has suggested that the anti-school subculture is not prevented by mixed ability teaching (e.g. Willis, 1977). The reason is almost certainly that disaffection results from the pupils' recognition that their status in the school is low, and that their achievements are considered less worthwhile and less important than those of academically brighter pupils. When pupils feel that they have been written off as examination prospects, it is hardly surprising that they respond in kind.

Disaffection is not the problem in primary schools or in the early years of secondary schools that it becomes in the final two years of compulsory schooling. The argument that special educational provision, within the ordinary school system or outside it, acts as a form of social control nevertheless remains valid with respect to younger pupils. 'Remedial' classes, as the Warnock Report pointed out, cater for a highly diverse range of pupils. For many of these pupils a major factor in their placement is their disruptive influence in classes in the mainstream.

In a sense this is not surprising. Teachers are rightly concerned about the progress of the majority. The curriculum cannot sensibly centre on pupils with special needs. Hence, removal of pupils with the most extreme needs is regarded as necessary not only for their own benefit, but also for the benefit of other pupils. Some of the 'sin-bins', or units and centres for disruptive pupils, that have sprung up over the last ten years in almost all l.e.a.'s are quite explicit in seeing their role in this light. Three of the school-based units studied in Sheffield, for example, opened with the clear aim of enabling teaching to continue in ordinary classes by removing trouble-makers. Any benefit to the pupils would be seen as a bonus (Galloway *et al.*, 1982*a*).

There are two problems in this seductive argument. The first is that special provision, both in ordinary and in special schools, is almost invariably portrayed to parents as being in their children's best interests. As Tomlinson (1981) and Ford *et al.* (1982) have documented, teachers and professionals in the support services can use a range of arguments to 'persuade' parents to accept what is proposed for their child. Except possibly in a few units for disruptive pupils, the motive behind placement in special provision is said to be the child's interests. Parents are left in no doubt that in rejecting this they will be rejecting what is best for their child. The reality, however, is that special provision exists as much to promote the interests of other pupils as those of the pupils who receive it.

The second point has already been mentioned. Pupils selected for special provision, both within ordinary schools and in special schools, come predominantly from working-class homes. In one study, indeed, there was little or no social class distribution in four school for maladjusted pupils, since virtually all the pupils investigated came from social classes IV and V on the Registrar General's five point scale (Ford *et al.*, 1982). It is also clear that amongst children from working-class homes, a disproportionate number comes from the most socially disadvantaged groups.

Additional points are that:

(1) Boys are over-represented compared with girls, by three to one in schools for the maladjusted (DES, 1975).
(2) Pupils from ethnic minorities are over-represented (e.g. Ford *et al.*, 1982); in addition, one-third of pupils in Sheffield's special schools for the maladjusted in 1979 were of Caribbean origin.
(3) Pupils presenting overtly disruptive behaviour problems are over-represented compared with withdrawn pupils.

In view of this evidence it becomes implausible to deny that special educational provision can act as a form of social control, removing troublesome pupils from the schools' mainstream. This does not imply that special provision is ineffective. We shall look in the next two chapters at the effectiveness of different forms of provision in ordinary schools. It does, however, imply that we must look with great caution at the use of supposedly objective tests and screening instruments which identify pupils for special help. It also implies that we must look even more carefully at more obviously subjective procedures which identify pupils on the basis of teachers' opinions about a child. Finally it implies that we must look for the 'hidden agenda' behind assessment. In the 1950s and 1960s many schools used tests to stream pupils into the D stream, where they were taught by the least experienced and least competent teachers. We have to ask whether attempts to identify children with special educational needs may not similarly constitute a disguised attempt to remove them from the mainstream curriculum.

School-based Assessment

The special needs of some children are recognised before they enter an infant school at age five. By far the majority of pupils discussed by Warnock, however, are not regarded as having any special needs before they start school. Identification occurs at some stage throughout their nursery, primary or secondary school career. In the case of pupils presenting behavioural problems there is a strong tendency for 'identification' to be age-related: the older the pupils the more likely they are to be regarded as having special needs. The rate of psychiatric disorder amongst adolescents is not substantially higher than amongst 10-year-olds (Rutter *et al.*, 1976). Hence, the increased proportion in secondary schools of pupils regarded as having special needs is not reflected in any obvious way in an increased need for specialist psychiatric help outside the school.

How, then, may teachers come to regard around 20 per cent of their pupils as having special educational needs? Assessment can take place at four levels. The first concerns the school's procedures for monitoring and recording the progress of all its pupils. These will identify some pupils whose progress and/or behaviour may be a source of concern. In the second stage teachers undertake their own more detailed assessment, in discussion with the child's parents. In the third stage the school seeks advice at an informal level with members of support services, such as educational psychologists, school medical officers and educational welfare officers. Finally, the head teacher seeks a formal assessment under the 1981 Act, intending that the l.e.a. should eventually issue a Statement determining the child's educational needs. We consider each level of assessment in turn.

Assessment Throughout the School

Assessment which cannot be used to help teachers plan effective work with their pupils has little value. It may, of course, show that everyone is making excellent progress. One hopes, though, that besides generating a cosy glow inside everyone concerned, the results have some relevance in planning future work. Thus two questions should be asked about a school's procedures for assessing its pupils' progress. The first is whether the results are, or can be, used. The second is what they are used for. To rephrase these questions: do pupils *and* teachers benefit from the exercise? Does the school provide more valuable and rewarding experiences as a result? The answers are not always reassuring.

Acquiring Special Needs

Special needs are usually discovered in school. The first stage in the process of discovery must therefore be the school's routine procedures for recording pupil's progress and/or for sorting them into groups. This can happen at an informal level, when a teacher finds something disturbing about a child. It may be that child's behaviour or his progress. It can also happen at an informal level when a parent, health visitor, educational welfare officer or psychologist passes some information to the teacher. The information will be intended to benefit the child, and may in fact do so.

Sometimes, however, by alerting teachers to possible problems it may make them expect these, and hence reduce the child's chance of achieving a normal start in the school.

Liaison between professionals is necessary. Its aim is to alert the teacher to issues of immediate relevance to the child's education. Thus, a teacher should be told if a child is liable to minor epileptic seizures which might otherwise be taken for doziness or inattentiveness. Educational psychologists and school medical officers, incidentally, are not infrequently disconcerted to find that this information is not passed to the class teacher when a child moves to a new school. Similarly, teachers should be told enough about the child's home to enable them to offer parents a constructive partnership. Most children have a change of teacher each year. Expecting each new teacher to discover afresh that, in the absence of carefully structured guidelines from the school, Johnny's parents will use their own inimical methods to 'help' him with school work, is clearly a misuse of time and resources.

On the other hand some of the information exchanged between professionals has less helpful effects. If Mrs Chapman has had a series of problems over children from the Brown family, it will not be very helpful for the educational welfare officer to remark in the last week of term: 'oh yes, and you'll be having the Green twins next term; they're first cousins to the Browns and if anything even worse!' Many adults can recall with resentment being expected at school to live up, or down, to the reputation of an older brother or sister or other relation.

The regular assessments which some schools carry out on their children's progress constitute another, more familiar, way of identifying those with special needs. Here, too the procedures carry their own risks. At best they misidentify a proportion of pupils. At worst they may help to create special needs which subsequently generate stress for teachers and pupils alike. Two illustrations follow, one taken from the primary and one from the secondary sectors.

Many primary schools assess their pupils' progress in reading with a graded word reading test (e.g. Schonell and Goodacre, 1974). Such tests measure a child's ability to recognise words in isolation from any meaningful context. Put crudely, they test the child's capacity to 'bark at print'. Yet word recognition is only one of the skills required in reading. Fluency and comprehension are also essential aspects of reading ability. Moreover, some pupils are reluctant to try to read words out of context. Inevitably, the test produces 'false positives' and 'false negatives', i.e. pupils who appear, on the basis of the results, to have special needs, but are in fact making reasonable progress, and vice versa. The danger lies in teachers using the test results to decide:

(1) who has special needs and
(2) what books each child 'ought' to be reading. This can cause great frustration when some children are expected to read books which they find difficult, and other books which they find too simple.

The use of group intelligence tests to screen children's ability is even more controversial. The New Zealand Council for Educational Research recently produced a Test of Scholastic Aptitudes (Reid *et al.*, 1981) which is widely used throughout New Zealand to allocate pupils into ability based streams on admission to secondary school. Nash (1983) has shown that the test discriminates efficiently between Maori pupils and white New Zealanders, effectively ensuring that the former are clustered in the lower streams. Disaffection amongst pupils in their last two years at school is as much of a problem in New Zealand as in Britain. The problem is greater amongst pupils from the lower ability bands, to which Maoris and other Polynesian pupils tend to be allocated. It does not require too much of a logical leap to conclude:

(1) That the test results are used to justify the initial streaming.
(2) That low stream pupils have a low status throughout the school.
(3) That the behavioural problems they subsequently present result from recognition of their low status in the eyes of teachers and of the school's local community.

Undoubtedly, any New Zealand survey of children with special needs would identify a disproportionate number of Maori pupils. The reasons are highly complex, and certainly cannot be placed at the door of the education system alone. There are adequate grounds nevertheless for believing that the education system contributes to their educationally disadvantaged status. The use of the Test of Scholastic Aptitudes for streaming purposes is an interesting illustration of how assessment can help to create problems which are subsequently seen as evidence of special educational need.

In Britain secondary schools in general are less firmly streamed than in New Zealand. Yet here too many secondary schools and some primary schools routinely use group intelligence tests to 'check' their pupil's progress. The tests are enthusiastically promoted by publishing companies, which stand to make large profits from their sale. An argument frequently put forward is that the tests identify the bright pupil who is underachieving. This would be more convincing if there was more evidence that they are in fact used for this purpose, and that such pupils received appropriate special educational help as a result. It is likely that for every pupil who is correctly identified, another is misidentified. One boy from a 'problem' family took the test immediately after a knock on the head in the playground. Soon after the lesson he was taken to hospital with concussion. Yet the results were quoted in the staff room as evidence of his dullness.

More seriously, the fact that tests are used may lead teachers to equate the tests with assessment of the child's needs. A child has special needs if he cannot cope with the school's curriculum. Obtaining a low score on an intelligence test is not, *per se* evidence of anything. The emphasis in assessment should be on the child's regular classroom progress. Anything which diverts attention from this is potentially misleading. Similarly, there must be doubts about the value of any test whose results cannot readily be used to plan a more appropriate programme of work with the child.

Monitoring Children's Progress

The procedures discussed so far have been 'norm referenced': children's scores are compared with the 'norms', or scores of pupils on whom the test was standardised. An alternative approach is criterion referenced assessment: children's progress is assessed by reference to some agreed criterion, with no attempt to compare their progress with that of other pupils.

A school's policy on reading can provide a good example of criterion referenced assessment. Library books can be colour coded according to reading age. Teachers can then establish a pupil's reading ability with reference to books in the library. An informal reading inventory can not only confirm the child's ability to read words in a book, but also monitor fluency and comprehension (e.g. Pumfrey, 1976).

Progress is assessed according to the level of difficulty the child experiences. Selection of books is based on the purpose of the particular book, and the amount of help available from teachers or parents. Reading at an independent level, children can tackle the book with enjoyment, understanding and accuracy. At an instructional level the child will grasp much of the content but will still need some help. At a frustration level the child will probably find the book aversive. With an adequate colour coding system, children can be guided to books of an appropriate level. The limitations in the annual test still prevalent in many schools, are largely overcome, and children who may have special needs are identified for further assessment.

Teachers may, however, still see the need for a more systematic way of monitoring their pupil's general progress using the principles of criterion-referenced assessment. Lindsay (1982) developed an Infant Rating Scale for use with children aged 5 to 7. This aimed to give teachers 'a straightforward, but comprehensive instrument which they might use in the classroom to help in the analysis of their children's strengths and weaknesses.' The scale could be used to alert teachers to unevennesses in their pupils' development, and hence to plan future work based on a clearer understanding of their needs. A strength of the scale, and of similar scales such as the Croydon Checklist (Bryans and Wolfendale, 1973) is that the process of filling it in requires systematic observation of the child's behaviour and progress. Norm-referenced testing, in contrast, relies exclusively on the child's performance in the testing session.

There is controversy on how far these principles can be extended into the older primary school and secondary years. The ideas behind criterion referenced assessment remain equally valid for older pupils, but the competitive nature of the public examination system presents a major obstacle in practice. Increasingly, however, teachers and politicians are recognising that pupils should be judged on their own achievements, rather than compared with those of others. The development of pupils' profiles in secondary schools reflects this concern, and is leading l.e.a.'s to review their procedures for assessing the achievements of school leavers.

Assessing Special Needs Within the School

A Hidden Agenda?

The starting point in any attempt to assess a child's special needs is that he has already been identified from the assessments or progress monitoring which teachers carry out routinely on all their pupils. Assessment of special needs does not, therefore, occur in a vacuum. Questions have been raised, and expectations created by what has gone before. This previous experience may create its own 'hidden agenda'. Galloway (1981) describes how the teacher of 8-year-old Dean had made up her mind about him:

> 'He's just ESN!' she told the weekly welfare meeting. 'He shouldn't be here; it's not fair to him and it's not fair to the other children.' Miss Arnold, though, was a teacher whose judgement was uncomplicated by such nebulous concepts as doubt. When her mind was made up, the head reflected wearily, nothing could shift her. (p. 57)

Thus, requests for a teacher's assessment are not necessarily based on the hope of information that will enable the school to cater more effectively for the child's special needs. This may be the stated reason, but there may also be other motives. The 'hidden agenda' may be to obtain information to justify transfer to a special school. Teachers sometimes feel that they must present a strong argument when putting a case to the school's educational psychologist.

The Parents' Contribution

The DES (1983) makes clear that parents should be closely involved at every stage of their child's assessment. The initial stage is clearly of immense importance, but will raise fundamental questions about the nature of home-school relationships in many schools in Britain. Barton and Moody (1981) quote an indictment by Peter Mittler (1978) on the lack of contact between special schools and parents. Yet everything Mittler says could apply equally to ordinary schools:

> . . . there are *many* schools where such a partnership has hardly begun, where parents have played *no* part in helping to assess the strengths and weaknesses of the child, far less been involved in the design and implementation of a teaching programme. There are children whose parents have *no* knowledge of the objectives set by teachers for their child, if indeed any objectives have been set at all, schools where there is *no* system of communication, such as home-school diaries, where there are *no* visits by teachers to the home and *only* yearly formal visits by parents to

the school. (Barton and Moody's emphasis). (p. 138)

Both the 1980 and the 1981 Education Acts appear to extend parents' rights to information about their children's schools and to consultation as to where and how their children should be educated. How far political intent is converted into educational practice remains to be seen. There are two related problems. The first is that terms such as 'parents as partners' are notoriously open to different interpretations by teachers and parents. The second is that teachers and parents may have radically conflicting ideas about the purpose of consultation. Crudely, consultation can be used by teachers to build up a dossier of information with highly ambiguous meanings.

The point is that parents and teachers may see the same incidents from different perspectives. The teacher may remark to an educational psychologist: 'I have seen the parents five times, and it's been obvious all along that they really don't appreciate Kevin's difficulties. They don't seem interested in any suggestions we make'. The parents' attitude is thus implicitly used to explain why the school cannot meet the child's undoubted special needs. The parents, though may say: 'We knew from the start that that teacher was against him. She called us into school time and again, just to show us what he was doing wrong and to criticise what we were doing at home'. From their conflicting perspectives, both parties are making valid statements. The trouble was that the teacher had a hidden agenda in consulting the parents. For their part, they sensed a lack of openness and reacted defensively.

Clearly, this does not happen in all schools. There are schools in which parents and teachers are able to find common ground, and to work together in identifying and meeting children's special needs at an early stage. The success of parent involvement in reading provides an encouraging implication that reading difficulties can be reduced when parents and teachers work together (Hewison and Tizard, 1980; Tizard *et al.*, 1982). In this particular example, teachers gave parents only very broad guidelines about how they should listen to their children reading. Communication, though, is a two-way process. Parents frequently have a pretty clear idea why their child is behaving badly or failing to make progress at school. Yet they may keep their views to themselves when visiting the school, either because their advice is not sought, or because they feel that criticism of teachers may rebound against their child.

Diagnostic Teaching and Testing

Teachers have access to a range of diagnostic tests, for example Daniels and Diack's (1958) Standard Reading Test, Neale's (1957) Analysis of Reading Ability or Gillham's (1980) Basic Number Diagnostic Test. Diagnostic tests aim to provide information which has immediate implications for future work with the child. Superficially, there is little point is carrying out diagnostic assessment unless the teacher can see some hope of using the results.

Sometimes, however, information derived from diagnostic testing may be useful in persuading a reluctant authority to provide additional resources in the form of books, materials or even additional staff. In effect, the school is demonstrating that they have evidence of children's special educational needs, know how to meet these needs, and would be able to do so with some additional help. If the l.e.a. fails to provide the resources requested, the head teacher can request a formal assessment under the 1981 Act.

This gives teachers a further opportunity to argue their case, with support from parents. The l.e.a. may thus find itself in the embarrassing position of having to issue a Statement specifying the child's need for special educational provision which it had previously, at an informal level, refused to provide. Rather than incur the trouble, expense and potential embarrassment of carrying out formal Assessments, the l.e.a. may decide to accede to requests for extra resources at the preliminary stage. There is little doubt that the 1981 Act may enable teachers to use the results of thorough school-based analyses of special needs to secure extra resources. It is unclear, though, how many head-teachers will be prepared to risk their chief education officer's displeasure by using it in this way.

While the possibilities for using diagnostic material in this 'political' way clearly exist, it will more frequently be used to plan work within the school's existing resources. The results are used to plan a teaching programme adapted to the child's needs. The teaching programme itself, however, should be used diagnostically. Diagnostic assessment of a child's reading skills, for example, may reveal adequate knowledge of phonic principles, but confusion over irregular words. A programme to teach the child the most frequently occurring irregular words using flash cards may result in little improvement, in which case the teacher will modify the programme, or change it. On the other hand, the programme may appear successful, but without accompanying improvement in the child's reading comprehension. In this case the teacher will need to think again about the reasons for the child's difficulties. In both cases, the teacher is using the special provision diagnostically, modifying the material to suit the situation in the light of the child's progress.

In this sense, of course, special educational provision is no different from ordinary teaching in the school's mainstream. It may be argued that *all* teaching is diagnostic in the sense that the teacher's preconceived ideas may stand in need of modification or alteration as children develop fresh interests, make faster progress or experience greater difficulty than the teacher had anticipated.

As a cautionary note, it is worth adding that not all children who appear to have special needs do in fact require special programmes based on diagnostic work. Sometimes a simple change of class can be helpful, as when there is a personality clash between a teacher and a pupil. From a senior teacher's point of view, transferring a pupil to another class has two implications. First, the child's progress must be carefully monitored in the new class, to see whether his needs are being met or merely disguised. Second, the child's problems may have identified problems in the attitude or professional skill of the original teacher. Hence, attempting to meet pupils' special needs has important consequences for staff training and development. (*See* Chapter 7).

The Educational Support Services

After carrying out their own assessment of a child's special needs the next stage is for teachers to consult the education support services. This is not required before requesting a formal assessment under the 1981 Act, but is widely regarded as good practice. The services of most obvious relevance are the l.e.a.'s psychological service and the school health service. In addition teachers may consult the educational welfare service and the l.e.a.'s advisers, or inspectors.

Before considering the constructive role which these services may play in assessing children's needs, it is again important to establish the existence of a possible hidden agenda. Ostensibly the reason for referral is the hope that the services concerned may be able:

(1) To clarify the nature of the child's special needs.
(2) To offer explanations for them.

(3) To help teachers meet the child's needs, i.e. to teach him more effectively.

The less obvious reason for referral is to initiate a process which will result in the child's removal from the school.

This is most likely to occur when the school has tried for some time to contain a problem, but refers to specialist services following a crisis which convinces teachers that some other form of provision is required. Murphy (1981, quoted by Welton *et al.*, 1982) noted that educational psychologists approached cases with an open mind as to how and where a child's needs should be met. This 'open-decision' starting point could conflict with that of teachers who had already decided that a change of school was necessary.

Welton *et al.* (1982) also implied that the child's needs were not the only factor in determining where and whether schools sought professional advice. Much also depended on the relationships which they had established with members of different support services. This relationship, as much as the nature of the child's problem, might determine who was first consulted.

A more complex point, discussed by Dessent (1983) concerns the nature of responsibility for meeting the child's needs. He explains:

> The vast majority of referrals to an educational psychologist can be regarded as questions along the lines of: 'Is this child our responsibility or someone else's' (special schools, remedial services, child guidance). Psychologists in most areas could easily list 'good' and 'bad' schools in terms of the schools' ability to cater for children with special needs. 'Good' schools are identified by the fact that the head and class teachers within the school assume personal and professional responsibility for teaching *all* children in their area rather than by the possession of any particular technical expertise, teaching approaches or methods of organisation. Such schools require dramatically less involvement from psychologists as definers of special needs . . . One quickly becomes aware as a psychologist that by simply visiting a school and talking to or listening to the teacher of a referred child you are often regarded as providing a useful service because in so doing the responsibility of the child is shared with you and often imperceptibly transferred to you! (p. 93)

This process happens with doctors even more than with educational psychologists. Teachers may say, with an obvious air of relief 'She's under Dr X now', implying that their own responsibility is thereby reduced, even though Dr X almost certainly has no training or expertise in meeting special educational needs.

It is important to be clear that this sharing of responsibility is not in itself either surprising or undesirable. Teaching is a stressful occupation at the best of times. Teaching children with special needs in ordinary schools is potentially rewarding, but also potentially extremely stressful. Teachers are fully justified if they feel that responsiblity for the children concerned should to some extent be shared with professionals who have had more specific training.

The important point is not the sharing of responsibility, so much as the scope of each person's activities. A teacher may say to an educational psychologist: Can you suggest some activities which I can use to help Helen learn to read? The teacher here is making clear that he retains responsibility for Helen's teaching. He is asking the psychologist to share responsibility for choice of activities. By implication, if the suggestions do not prove successful the teacher and the psychologist can together work out some other approach. This is quite different from saying: 'We've already done everything possible for Helen in this school, so now we're referring her to you'. Here, the teacher is explicitly passing responsibility for the child to the psychologist, effectively absolving himself from further involvement.

What, then, is the most constructive role for members of the support services, working in partnership with teachers? Experience suggests that they can fulfil four related functions.

(1) They can provide an independent view of the child's needs. Precisely because they are not working with the child on a day-to-day basis, they should have greater objectivity, and see the child's difficulties from a broader perspective.
(2) They should have knowledge of good practice in other schools in the l.e.a., and of national trends. This knowledge should enable them to disseminate ideas, and put teachers in touch with colleagues with relevant experience both in special and in ordinary schools.
(3) They should have access to other sources of help, for the school, the child or the family. Further, they should be able to advise on the need for more specialised investigations.
(4) They have specialised training enabling them to contribute to a comprehensive assessment of the child's needs. Since the

needs of some children reflect a complex interaction between medical, psychological, educational and social factors, it is logical that assessment should be multi-disciplinary.

The final point does not imply that schools should always seek advice from a school doctor, an educational psychologist and an educational welfare officer. The psychologist and doctor contribute routinely to formal assessments under the 1981 Act, but we are still talking here about the school's decision to seek further advice at an informal level in carrying out its own internal assessment of the child's needs. As suggested already, in practice schools turn to the professional with whom they have the best relationships. Setting these personal factors aside, how should members of each profession be able to contribute to an understanding of each child's needs?

Educational psychologists are trained teachers with a first degree in psychology and an advanced qualification in the applications of psychology in education and in child development. A substantial part of their work has always been to advise on children's special educational needs, and the 1981 Act for the first time requires l.e.a.'s to consult them before issuing a Statement, and hence before placing a child in a separate special school. Among educational psychologists there has been increasing doubt about the value of spending most of their time in individual assessments. Recognising the school's influence on its children's behaviour and progress, many members of the profession have been exploring ways to extend their work in schools (e.g. Gillham, 1978; Sheffield Psychological Service, 1981; Cox and Lavelle, 1982).

In addition critics from outside the profession have drawn attention to ways in which educational psychologists act as agents of social control, removing troublesome pupils out of the school's mainstream (e.g. Tomlinson, 1981; Sewell, 1981). Whatever members of the profession may prefer, however, there is little doubt that the 1981 Act will require them to spend more time on individual assessment rather than less. As Goodwin's (1983) work shows, educational psychologists may have an ideological commitment to meeting special needs in ordinary schools, but in practice they can do little to resist increasing demands for separate provision.

The 1981 Act poses two challenges for the profession. The first is to find practical ways to resist demands for separate provision —

demands which the Act's lip service to integration will do nothing to reduce. The second is 'to develop their understanding of the social psychology and sociology of schools, and to integrate this into their traditional interests in children's learning processes and psychosocial development' (Galloway, 1982*c*, p. 12). For teachers, the challenge is to see educational psychologists, not as the special school gate-keeper, but rather as a potential resource in helping them to identify children's special needs and to provide suitable teaching programmes.

The role of school medical officers contains fewer inherent contradictions than that of educational psychologists. As part of the l.e.a.'s special needs bureaucracy, psychologists are divided between loyalty to their clients, namely children and parents, and the demands of teachers who implicitly expect them to serve the school, or the l.e.a. Since the child's needs are *not* always the same as those of the school, the dilemma is insoluble. School doctors, on the other hand are not employed directly by the l.e.a. and hence retain greater independence. Their brief, moreover, is more specific than that of educational psychologists. Although they still carry out some medical screening, one of their primary responsibilities is to advise teachers on the educational implications of a child's medical condition. If a child is known to have minor epileptic seizures, for example, the teacher will need advice on what action, if any, is required. Similarly the teacher of a child with some hearing loss requires guidance on what the child can, and cannot, be expected to hear.

The educational welfare service has traditionally been responsible for investigating cases of poor school attendance, and taking appropriate action to arrange return to school. Since the Ralphs Report on the role and training of educational welfare officers, the service has gradually developed a wider brief (Local Government Training Board, 1972). Educational welfare officers in many l.e.a.'s now hold a social work qualification, and see their role in terms of preventive social work. Certainly, they are in a much better position than social workers employed by a Social Services Department to offer families help before their problems become acute (Fitzherbert, 1977*a*, 1977*b*). In the assessment of children with special needs, e.w.o.'s may be able:

(1) To advise teachers on the educational implications of stress the child may be experiencing at home;

(2) To advise parents on welfare benefits to which they may be entitled and sources of professional help over problems that may exist in the home.

Formal Assessments and Statements Under the 1981 Act

Overview

Formal assessment may be seen as a safety net, fulfilling three functions:

(1) Protecting parents' rights to involvement in educational decisions about their child.
(2) Protecting children's rights to a suitable educational programme based on a comprehensive assessment of their special needs.
(3) Protecting teachers' rights to adequate resources to cater effectively for children with special needs, whether in an ordinary school or a special school.

In an ideal world formal assessment should seldom be needed. Children presenting behaviour problems would no longer be sent to special schools for the maladjusted and children with moderate learning difficulties would no longer be sent to special schools formerly classified as catering for the ESN(M). Instead, the needs of both groups would be catered for in ordinary schools. Children with other disabilities would also be educated in ordinary schools, though the specialised needs of some children would clearly require teaching facilities separate from the school's mainstream. The DES (1983) guidelines imply that formal Statements would be required only in respect of this latter group. L.e.a.'s such as Oxfordshire, which are integrating many pupils formerly classified as ESN(M) in ordinary schools without issuing Statements, have so far not attracted censure from the DES. In theory, therefore, Statements based on formal assessments should seldom be required in l.e.a.'s which are committed in practice as well as in theory to integration.

The position is not, however, altogether straightforward. If relationships between teachers, parents, professionals in the support services and administrators are good, Statements should indeed seldom be needed. The reason is simply that in such circumstances everyone concerned would be aiming to meet the child's special needs in the ordinary school system. Unfortunately relationships sometimes fall short of this ideal. In such cases Statements are designed to protect the interests of the different people concerned. Yet it is precisely in such circumstances that they are least likely to be effective. To understand why we need to consider why it has always been such a straightforward matter to persuade parents to accept special education for their children, and how ordinary schools may react to the issue of a Statement on their own pupils.

Referral to special schools for the ESN(M) or the maladjusted generally follows a long period of failure in the ordinary school. Parents may be profoundly unhappy about the prospect of separate special schooling, yet they may be even unhappier about the existing school's inability or unwillingness to meet their child's needs. All too easily, special schooling can become a form of 'Hobson's Choice'.

In theory, the 1981 Act can change this. A Statement can specify that the child should remain in his existing school, and define the special educational provision that must be made for him there. This conveniently overlooks two problems. The first is that no-one can legislate for teacher commitment. If teachers resent, or are indifferent to the child's presence, the outlook is bleak. In practice children are referred to special schools because their teachers find their progress and/or behaviour disturbing. Statements can require these children to remain in ordinary schools, but will not necessarily persuade teachers that this is desirable. If this happens, it will be a simple matter for teachers to argue at the annual review required by the Act that the child has 'failed to respond' to the special help that has been provided.

The second problem concerns the way ordinary schools may decide to cater for children with special needs in general, and with Statements in particular. Administratively, the easiest solution is to create a Department for Children with Special Needs. Here children may in theory pursue a curriculum designed specifically to meet their individual needs. In practice they may be separated from the curriculum in the mainstream, with little prospect of return. Tomlinson (1982) believes that the 1981 Act will result in larger numbers of pupils being separated from the mainstream curriculum. In practice, she argues, the Act:

> . . . will mean that large numbers of mainly working class and black children will be segregated in special units or classes and thus officially be placed in special education, albeit as non-

recorded children on whom the l.e.a. does not 'maintain a Statement'. In terms of the normal goals of the school that they attend, they will be offered a 'non-education', which will fit them only for low-status employment or unemployment. (p. 177).

Although Tomlinson is referring here to children without Statements in ordinary schools, there is every reason to suppose that the danger is even more acute for those with the dubious 'protection' of a Statement.

Conclusions

Ostensibly, the aim of assessment is to identify the child's special educational needs and to help teachers to meet them as appropriately as possible. The fact that a 'hidden agenda' is possible does not mean that it necessarily exists. The evidence suggests that some schools are highly successful in working with pupils who they recognise as having special educational needs. These schools also contain pupils who present few obvious problems, but who would undoubtedly be regarded as having special needs if they attended a different school. In other words, factors within the school are as relevant in assessing a child's special needs as factors within the child and the family.

Both the Warnock Report and the 1981 Act emphasise the importance of individual assessment. The necessity for investigating the child's needs as an individual is not disputed. Individual identity, though is established in a social context. Assessment which does not present information about the child in the context of educational and social experiences at school is at best one-sided. At worst it is dangerously misleading, by causing teachers, other professionals and even parents to individualise the problem, locating it firmly in the child, rather than seeing it as the product of wider factors. Assessment is a necessary step on the path to meeting a child's special needs. Yet it can also contribute to these needs. To see how this happens we need to consider the provision that schools can make for children with learning and behaviour problems.

4 POLICY AND PROVISION FOR CHILDREN WITH LEARNING PROBLEMS

Introduction

In this chapter we shall be discussing ways in which individual schools, assisted by the l.e.a. through its stated policy and through its support services, may plan effective work with children with special needs. We shall give some emphasis to provision for children with learning problems, as issues dealing specifically with recent developments for behaviourally disturbing pupils are dealt with in the next chapter. There is, however, considerable overlap between the two groups, which is reflected in both chapters. This chapter starts with an analysis of some implications of Warnock's concept of special need for the organisation of teaching in ordinary schools. We then look briefly at the research evidence on the results of special and remedial education before considering alternatives open to l.e.a.s and to individual schools. The twin emphases are on the possibilities opened up by the 1981 Act, and on the way its aims may be subverted in practice.

The Range of Special Needs

The Warnock Committee was never in any doubt about the diversity of the 20 per cent of pupils said to be in need of special educational help at some stage in their school career. Nor was the Committee in any doubt about the diversity in the pupils who had traditionally remained in ordinary schools, with or without formal special educational provision being made for them. Indeed it was this very diversity which led the Committee to criticise the term remedial (*see* DES, 1978*a*, p. 47).

At one extreme there are children who could be regarded as candidates for special schools for the ESN(M). The criteria for admission to these schools had always been haphazard, depending at least as much on the availability of places, on the pupil's behaviour and on the teacher's attitude to the pupil, as on measured intelligence or educational attainment. All ordinary schools have always

contained pupils whose measured IQ and attainments would undoubtedly have justified special education if their head teachers
had pressed for it hard enough.

At the other extreme are the so-called gifted pupils who may also
experience enormous frustration if expected to work at the same
level and speed as their peers. The child who can cope without difficulty with 8 'O' levels at 13 and 3 'A' levels at 14, without sacri-
ficing the other curriculum areas implicit in a balanced, liberal
education has special needs as obvious as those of the most
backward pupil. The special needs most frequently found between
these extremes are those of:

(1) Pupils whose relatively low academic attainments cannot
    meaningfully be said to indicate underachievement.
(2) Pupils whose poor attainments are associated with absence
    from school because of illness, frequent change of teacher or
    of school, family disruption or some other social factors.
(3) Pupils with a specific learning difficulty; the most widely
    discussed of these is dyslexia; though the usefulness of the
    term has been sharply criticised (e.g. Yule *et al.*, 1974; DES,
    1972) the existence of the learning difficulties relating
    specifically to reading is not in dispute; a similar situation
    exists with respect to mathematical ability (e.g. Lansdown,
    1978).

Of these groups, probably the largest is that of so-called slow-
learning and ESN(M) pupils. This statement is made on the basis of
the statistical assumptions inherent in the way tests of intelligence
and educational attainment are constructed. By definition, any test
succeeding in covering the full ability range will identify a proportion of slow learners. The size of the proportion depends not on the
test but on the cut-off point selected by the teacher or researcher.

It is clear nevertheless that the diversity of special needs requires
a similar diversity in educational provision. The Statement based
on a formal assessment under the 1981 Act lends statutory support
to the principle that special educational provision should be based
on a thorough analysis of the individual's needs. There would seem
to be no logical reason for thinking that such a diverse group of
children could sensibly be catered for in a single class or even in
classes within a single special needs department in a secondary
school. If the children are spread throughout the school, then it

follows that provision for them should likewise be spread throughout the school.

This argument by-passes the twin objections:

(1) That slow-learning pupils who cannot realistically be said to be underachieving might be thought to require a modified curriculum and syllabus, separate from the mainstream.
(2) That pupils with specific learning difficulties, for example in reading, require intensive remediation in small classes specifically designed with their needs in mind.

These are attractive arguments, easily used to justify removing the pupils in question from ordinary classes where their presence disturbs the teacher, and may affect the progress of the majority. We need, therefore, to look briefly at the research evidence on these children's progress in ordinary and in special classes.

The Evidence for Mainstream Provision for Children with Learning Difficulties

Ordinary Class or Special Class?

We have already noted Tomlinson's (1982) suggestion that the 1981 Education Act may increase the number of pupils educated in special education departments following a separate curriculum from that of other pupils. In the past, debate has centred on whether the pupils concerned made better progress in ordinary schools or in special schools. This, however, is an over-simplification. The real question is whether they make better progress in ordinary classes, or in special classes, irrespective of whether these special classes are in a special school or in an ordinary school. Although full-time 'remedial' classes have often been seen as part of an ordinary school's provision for its pupils, they may have incorporated many of the characteristics of the separate special school.

Galloway and Goodwin (1979) reviewed early American studies suggesting that the educational progress of slow-learning children was better if they remained in ordinary schools than if they transferred to special schools. The position with respect to social adjustment was more complicated. Some studies suggested that children at special schools were happier at school than children remaining in ordinary schools. An important Scandinavian study of low-attaining children in ordinary schools, however, suggested that children educated in ordinary classes made better educational progress and were happier at home than children in special classes. The special class children, on the other hand appeared happier at school (Osterling, 1967).

More recently, Carlberg and Kavale (1980) reviewed 50 studies comparing children placed in special and in ordinary classes. The general impression from these studies was that slow-learners and ESN(M) pupils suffered from placement in special classes by comparison with their peers of similar measured ability remaining in the mainstream. The authors concluded that there was 'no justification for placement of low IQ children in special classes'.

Virtually all the comparison studies suffer from methodological problems. Wherever special classes exist, there is pressure to fill them with the worst or most disturbing cases. Consequently, it is difficult to compare like with like, since the special class group may have presented more severe problems, or have been living in less favourable family circumstances in the first place. The consistency of the findings is nevertheless impressive, and has been further demonstrated within a secondary school by Frampton (1981). This small-scale study in New Zealand compared the progress of pupils in a traditional slow-learner class with the progress of pupils admitted to the same school the following year, when the slow-learners were integrated into the mainstream. Her main conclusion provides a good summary of all the research in this area:

> All other things being equal, it appears that low ability pupils can be expected to make about as much progress in ordinary classes as they can be expected to make in a separate slow learner class. Since this finding is consistent with the results of a number of other studies of the same question, there seems little point in suggesting that the question be made the subject of further research. (p. 11).

This conclusion is legitimate as far as it goes. There is very little point in continuing to debate whether these pupils suffer from integration into ordinary classes in the mainstream. The evidence is quite clear that they do not. All the same, a number of disturbing questions remain. One concerns the effect on other pupils of increasing the ability range within a class. A second concerns the effect of part-time withdrawal groups offering special educational help with specific problems. A third concerns nature of support and training that should be offered to teachers in the mainstream when the ability range of pupils in their classes is extended. The evidence may suggest that the low ability pupils do not suffer, but teachers have every reason to object that this not only implies complacency, but also lack of sensitivity to their own concerns.

'Remedial' Teaching

There seems little doubt that children frequently make quite rapid progress when they receive part-time 'remedial' help. Reviews of the literature also indicate, though, that this progress is frequently lost if support is not maintained on return to the mainstream (e.g. Sampson, 1975; Galloway and Goodwin, 1979). At one level, this is not in the least surprising. As Cashdan and Pumphrey (1969) argued, if the situation in the pupil's ordinary class had contributed to his need for help, returning to an unchanged situation would imply a high probability of regression.

Their argument was that children should receive continuing remedial help while attending ordinary classes. Another approach would consider the possibility of providing additional support and resources to mainstream teachers. This might enable them to maintain the progress achieved in a remedial group, or to avoid the necessity for part-time withdrawal in the first place.

On theoretical grounds, part-time withdrawal classes raise similar questions to full-time remedial classes. Part-time classes are generally smaller, and hence are better equipped, in principle, to base a teaching programme on the child's individual needs. Because they are smaller, they need not contain the extraordinarily diverse range of learning and behavioural problems frequently found in full-time remedial classes. On the other hand their size and the potentially individual nature of their activities carry their own problems. Children are referred for special educational help because they have been failing in an ordinary class. It seems illogical, therefore, to provide intensive individual or small-group help if this is not directly linked to the mainstream curriculum.

In this sense, the questions about the effects of part-time remedial classes, progress of 'ordinary' pupils and the training needed by teachers in the mainstream are all linked. The evidence does not suggest that childen of average ability and above suffer from the ability range being extended to include children with special needs; indeed since the abolition of the 11 plus, virtually all primary school classes have contained the full ability range. No startling evidence has been produced that mixed ability classes in this age group militate against the interests of the highest ability pupils (e.g. Barker Lunn, 1970). The question nevertheless remains contentious and in secondary schools is aggravated by the complexity of ability banding and setting arrangements. In many schools integrating slow-learning pupils will mean putting them in the 'B' band for general subjects, perhaps with further ability setting in specific subjects such as maths. Whatever arrangements are made, they will have implications for teachers throughout the school and for the school's curriculum. It is to this that we must now turn.

The Mainstream Curriculum

In discussing ways to meet special educational needs in ordinary schools it is conventional to consider how the curriculum may be made accessible to all pupils. An equally reasonable question is how far special needs are created where the curriculum is not accessible. This question is independent of the organisation of special educational provision within a school, whether on a separate special class basis, part-time withdrawal or support within ordinary lessons. What Warnock calls full functional integration, i.e. pupils with special needs working alongside their peers in ordinary classes, does nothing in itself to ensure that the curriculum is accessible. Children can fail just as badly in an ordinary class as in a special class. Conversely, a separate class may, in theory, link its curriculum very closely with the mainstream, creating ample opportunity for successful return. The question, rather, is how failure can be created in the curriculum, irrespective of who caters for the children's needs and where.

Teacher and Pupil Expectations

A boy at a residential school for the maladjusted once told me that he could not help his bizarre behaviour because he was maladjusted. Pupils with low attainments in primary and secondary schools use other terms to describe themselves or their peers. Perhaps the most common are 'dim' or 'thick'. The pupil's self image is generally linked to the teacher's expectations. At the residential school there was occasionally concern that a new boy behaved quite normally. Staff felt he was unable to show his real problems. When his behaviour started to deteriorate there was a feeling of relief that he now felt 'safe' enough to show his 'real' problem! Although extreme, this is not so very far removed from the way that teachers in ordinary schools sometimes regard pupils believed to have a low IQ or other learning difficulties. The point is that failure can be created by the teacher's expectations (*see*, for example, Pidgeon, 1970; Downey, 1977; Nash, 1978).

Curriculum Resources

Failure also becomes inevitable when teachers lack the knowledge or the resources to adapt the curriculum to their pupils' needs. In our study of pupils suspended from school we found that two-thirds had a reading age three years below their chronological age and three-quarters a reading age two years below. The mean verbal scale IQ was 82, with over 20 per cent obtaining score of 70 or lower (Galloway, 1982*b*). Looking at these pupils' experiences at school, it became clear that for many of them a return to school would involve a return to a daily diet of educational failure. The problem was not, essentially, that they had been taught in ordinary classes or in separate remedial classes, so much as the nature of their experiences in these classes. In this respect pupils who were suspended merely represented the tip of the ice-berg, since many more pupils were also deriving little benefit or satisfaction from school, even though they had not presented such severe problems.

Two of the innumerable factors contributing to curriculum failure are the reading age required by text books, and a tendency to teach to the needs of the middle-range of pupils. Some maths and science textbooks, in particular, are notorious for requiring reading ability well above the average for the children using them. Since books cannot be changed at will, this has obvious implications for in-service education throughout the school. These implications were fully recognised by the Bullock Report (DES, 1976) with its concept of language across the curriculum. They provide an excellent illustration of the ways in which the education of children with special needs is intricately linked with development of literacy in all curriculum areas and for all pupils.

It also becomes clear from this example that in talking about meeting children's needs we are also talking about teachers' needs. Complex or inappropriate language in a text book is a potential source of failure for pupils. So is membership of a class where the teacher 'teachers to the middle', with the result that half the pupils are bored or frustrated, and behave accordingly. Yet the pupils' failure increases experience of stress and reduces job-satisfaction for the teachers. The question therefore, is not simply what separate provision, full-time or part-time, is needed to meet pupils' needs. An even more important question concerns the training, continuing support and resources needed to enable teachers to provide a curriculum and a climate which recognises and meets the range of abilities present in the classroom. This does not, of course, imply that all children should be working to the same level, but rather that the curriculum should not make failure inevitable for any child.

Whose Responsibility?

An obvious implication of this analysis is that teachers in the mainstream retain responsibility for the curriculum, and for adapting it to meet special educational needs. Yet although they retain responsibility, they should expect practical support and guidance from colleagues with specialised experience in assessing pupils' special needs and planning programmes for them. There is an analogy here in the relationship between teachers with specific responsibility for special needs and members of the support services such as educational psychologists.

We have already noted that referral sometimes seems to imply transfer of responsibility for the child to the psychologist from the teacher. Misunderstandings occur when psychologists implicitly reject this assumption, regarding their role as helping the teacher to work with the pupil. In the same way, class teachers and subject teachers are sometimes only too eager to pass responsibility for a child with learning or behaviour problems to the special needs or remedial specialist. Such transfers of responsibility are seldom expressed openly. Precisely because they are seldom expressed openly they can become a source of great tension in a school which is pursuing a policy of integration.

As in the relationship between teachers responsible for special needs and eductional psychologists the implication is clear. The onus rests on the specialists to define their areas of responsibility, making clear where their responsibility starts and finishes. In so doing, they also define the limits to the class or subject teacher's responsibility. This aims to minimise if not prevent friction or misunderstanding, though the scope of each persons's responsibility will still be open to debate.

The special needs department, for example, may offer to help members of the English department prepare work cards and other activities which enable them to cater more adequately for pupils across the whole ability range. The English department may reply: 'that's all very well, but how much time will we have to spend on this, and how do we organise a class of 30 so that we have time to spend ensuring that the special needs kids understand how to use these materials?' The reply reveals problems both of motivation and of professional technique. The teachers are concerned about the time needed to prepare materials, and about ways to use the materials in the classroom.

In primary schools the situation is even more complex. The special needs 'specialist', if such a person exists at all, may well be a part-time teacher with no particular training or expertise for the job. The 1981 Education Act with its lip service to the notion of educating children with special needs in ordinary schools will do little or nothing to reduce the tendency on the part of administrators and head teachers to regard part-time 'remedial' staff as a prime target for cuts in expenditure. If a primary school does have a teacher with responsibility for special needs, the teacher concerned will have to sort out problems of accountability and responsibility with the school's class teachers. Here too there may be problems both of motivation and of professional technique.

The problem of motivation is certainly the most important. There is now ample evidence that teachers can work effectively with children with special needs, given the will and professional support. The type of responsibility proposed for specialists does, however, have important implications for their status throughout the school. We are arguing that they should not take personal responsibility, but rather that they should be seen as co-ordinating and facilitating the work of mainstream teachers. To do this requires an active partnership with teachers throughout the school. Working with children with special needs has to be seen as an integral part of all teachers' professional responsibilities. This will not be achieved without the active support and commitment of the head and senior staff. Nor will it be achieved unless the teacher with responsibility for special needs in a primary school and the head of the special needs department in a secondary school are recognised as having the necessary status. Simply giving the head of department a special allowance equivalent to that of the head of a major subject department such as English or Maths is not in itself enough to ensure his status. Yet without such a post the special needs department is seen throughout the school to be subordinate to the main subject areas. Inevitably, the special needs teachers are then at a crippling disadvantage when negotiating the nature of special provision that should be offered to a child in an ordinary class.

While reactions within individual schools are obviously critical, the l.e.a.'s policy also exerts an important influence on the priority special needs receive in schools. L.e.a.'s, as we argued in the last chapter, can conform to the Act's bureaucratic detail while ignoring its spirit. Yet l.e.a.'s themselves are not entirely free agents. We need now to consider the influence of l.e.a. policy and the constraints on it.

LEA Support for Special Educational Needs

Demand and Supply

One of the paradoxes facing local councillors and l.e.a. administrators is that growing expertise in meeting special needs in ordinary schools is not matched by a corresponding reduction in the demand for special school places. There are two explanations. One is that as teachers in ordinary schools develop greater expertise they become more aware of, and sensitive to, their own shortcomings. In other words, their increased knowledge and understanding makes them realise how much more could be achieved, given the time and resources. In these circumstances it is not surprising that they should look to the 'experts' in special schools to take responsibility for children whose needs they feel unable to meet. The fact that the 'experts' seldom have greater expertise than they do themselves is either unrecognised or overlooked.

The second explanation is more complex, and concerns the sense of loyalty which teachers feel to their own school or their own professional groups. Special school staff have an understandable commitment to the value of what they can offer. This commitment, however, is sometimes based on an explicit rejection of the values which they perceive as dominant in ordinary schools.

In New Zealand we described pupils and teachers in one form of special education in New Zealand as 'refugees from school' (Galloway and Barrett, 1982). The pupils spoke with bitter resentment about their experiences in ordinary schools, describing examples of unfairness from staff and persistent failure in the curriculum. Yet when teachers were asked why they had entered special education, many of them gave explanations which were strikingly similar to those of the pupils. The pupils had been sent to a separate centre, but recalled their mainstream schooling with bitterness. The teachers had opted for posts in separate special education, because they had reacted against precisely the problems about which their pupils were complaining. Informal discussion suggests that this rejection of the values of ordinary schools is not uncommon in special school teachers. If so, it is hardly surprising that l.e.a.'s face formidable obstacles in developing a coherent policy of educating children with special needs in ordinary schools. Parallel systems operating in ordinary schools and special schools become almost inevitable, each with its own management structure and ethos. The management structure and ethos is reflected at County Hall as much as in the staffrooms and classrooms of the l.e.a.'s schools. In a perceptive passage N. Jones (1983) argues:

> Parallelism comes in many forms and guises. It effects such minor details as who draws up the advertisements for new special needs staff, who short lists, who is on the interview panels, and where the authority for the final choice of candidate is posited. Of more major importance it poses the question of who is accountable at advisory level for the new teachers in the sectors who will be specialized in areas of learning difficulty: the county primary adviser who has responsibility for the peripatetic remedial services or the special need adviser under whose auspices the new staff are appointed according to one interpretation of the Warnock recommendation that 'remedial' should not be separated from 'special'? (pp. 70 – 1)

Conflict Between Policy and Practice

It was perhaps failure to grapple with these issues that caused the apparent problems in Sheffield's policy of integration. Goodwin (1983) documents the failure of formal l.e.a. policy, educational psychologists and a support teacher service to halt, or even reduce the flow of admissions to separate special schools. She considers the evidence:

> . . . hardly surprising, however, when taken in the context of the already well-established special school sector in the city. Even if

all the support services saw their role as change-agents, the inertia and vested interests they combat make it an unequal match. (p. 164)

In this context it is instructive that while committed in theory to a policy of integration, carrying out considerable reorganisation of special education resources, Sheffield Education Committee was in fact opening new special education facilities separate from the mainstream. These were a special school for maladjusted pupils and a centre for disruptive teenagers. The school for the maladjusted was residential, the ultimate in segregated provision. Moreover, the centre for disruptive pupils was terminal, with little prospect of pupils returning to ordinary schools. These developments, apparently so inconsistent with the Education Committee's stated policy on integration, were made possible by the lack of a co-ordinated plan to implement Committee policy towards special educational needs. Special education, meaning in practice special schools, remained administratively separate from ordinary primary and secondary schools. In seeking the committee's approval for a new special school the officer concerned could argue that:

(1) The pupils' needs had been demonstrated by their referral, and by head teachers' insistence that they could not be met at their existing school.
(2) The l.e.a. had a duty to make 'appropriate' provision for these pupils.

Oddly, the centre for disruptive pupils was administratively separate from special schools, coming under the general aegis of the officer responsible for secondary schools. He was able to argue to the committee that the centres were needed to cater for pupils who had been suspended from school, or who were in imminent danger of suspension and could not be catered for in the existing special schools.

Decisions about special education, then, were made on an *ad hoc* basis. They reflected:

(1) The priorities and interests of particular individuals.
(2) The lack of a co-ordinated approach to special educational needs, extending across existing administrative boundaries in the l.e.a..

(3) The Education Committee's reluctance to grapple with the practical implications of its own policy. These implications were not reflected in the scope of responsibilities given to the l.e.a.'s special education section nor in the status of the officer responsible for special education relative to that of the officer responsible for primary or secondary schools.

In retrospect, then, the inconsistency between theory and practice became predictable.

The difficulties in Sheffield illustrate a problem which faces developments of any kind. Change threatens the stability of an organisation, whether at school level or at the level of the l.e.a. Inevitably, there are people who fear the impact which change will have on their own lives and job satisfaction. Meeting special educational needs in ordinary schools has quite revolutionary implications for teachers in all sectors of education. Inevitably, change will be resisted. Just as inevitably, apparently sound educational reasons will be put forward to justify resistance, not least of which will be the supposedly detrimental effect on the pupils themselves. The problem lies in creating a climate favourable to change, not in demonstrating from research that new ideas have been successful elsewhere. An l.e.a. which lacks a coherent plan for implementing its stated policy has little hope of eliciting the support of sceptical head teachers. For their part, head teachers who lack a coherent policy will have little chance of convincing sceptical colleagues that they should increase their work-load by taking responsibility for children with special needs.

Special Units

This becomes even more of a problem when the l.e.a.'s integration policy involves setting up units in an ordinary school. The units come under the same administrative umbrella as special schools, and are seen as catering for the same pupils. In other words, 'locational integration' is achieved by shifting the place where special education is provided from a separate school to a unit in an ordinary school.

For some children with severe physical or intellectual disabilities, this can be an important step forward. Some of them will always require highly specialised teaching that cannot realistically be provided in the mainstream. A unit based in an ordinary school is potentially a valuable source of contact with non-handicapped children. It may also provide children in the school's mainstream with valuable social experience of contact with disabled children. How well it can work with children formerly regarded as ESN(M) is more problematic.

The existence of a unit set up to cater for ESN(M) pupils establishes the parallelism to which N. Jones (1983) refers. At the Cooper School, for example, there was separate provision both for ESN(M) and for 'remedial' pupils, each with its own head of department. The head of the ESN(M) unit found it hard to see how the curriculum offered to each group differed, and pointed out: 'when the pupils attended mainstream lessons — often supported by either the "special" or "remedial" teachers — they were taught from the same syllabus as the mainstream pupils, and they all belonged to mainstream tutor groups' (Garnett, 1983).

This anomaly did not prevent successful attempts to integrate ESN(M) and 'remedial' pupils at the Cooper School. It seems however, that successful integration may have been achieved in spite of l.e.a. policy rather than with its help. Garnett describes the tensions which can arise:

> Traditional remedial departments often appear to see the attachment of a special unit as a threat to their own position in the school. They do not generally view themselves as 'special educators' although they are likely to defend the notion that their pupils usually require a different kind of curriculum from those in the mainstream. That difference is not clearly defined but the adapted curriculum is certainly narrower. The pupils are identified as 'slow-learners' but not 'handicapped'. The latter children are thought to need yet another kind of curriculum. The fact that in essence the curricula observed to be offered in the different settings seem to be little different in terms of their aims, objectives and content is not always recognised. (p. 127)

Garnett also points out that mainstream teachers can have similar attitudes, regarding children with learning difficulties as the responsibility of remedial or special teachers. Such attitudes can, of course, occur anywhere. They are an occupational hazard facing all teachers with responsibility for children with special educational needs. L.e.a. policy cannot prevent their expression. It can, however, help to create a climate which inhibits it.

Developments in Scotland

Perhaps the best example of this comes from Scotland. Development was initiated by an HMI report criticising remedial provision based principally on teaching basic skills in full-time remedial classes or withdrawal groups (Scottish Education Department, 1978). In this report HMI argued that up to 50 per cent of pupils might have some learning difficulty, and that teachers should accept responsibility for them. Withdrawal of pupils from ordinary lessons was seen as a last resort, to be replaced by wide-ranging developments within the mainstream. These included particular attention to the transfer from primary to secondary schools, an increase in mixed ability teaching and as wide a range of curriculum options for the least able as for the most able.

HMI took the view that head teachers should have general responsibility for the education of children with learning difficulties, but that remedial specialists should be appointed to take major responsibility for implementing the necessary changes. In putting the proposals into practice much clearly depended on the lead from the l.e.a. The first necessity was a senior administrator with overall responsibility for encouraging the necessary developments. Booth (1983) summarised the process in two l.e.a.s.

> In Fife a depute director of education said, 'instead of debating its contents we decided to work out how to do something about it'. They set annual targets and established curriculum committees in the schools. By August 1981 they abolished all separate remedial classes and by August 1982 aimed to reduce the number of different teachers for first-year pupils in secondary schools, to introduce block time-tabling and to increase the emphasis on project work.
>
> In Grampian; which was one of the areas on which the HMI report was based, the depute director for secondary education had the job of co-ordinating developments in remedial provision. (p. 51)

This depute director was in no doubt that his job was not just to co-ordinate developments, but to initiate and guide them too:

> I have no doubt that it's my job as an official to make recommendations to the Education Committee after appropriate

consultation and then produce broad policy guidelines. Remedial education is a good example. Within certain guidelines you are free to exercise your own professional judgement but there are certain things you must not do, you must not have a separate class for remedial youngsters. (p. 51).

In his account of these developments in Scotland Booth makes clear that they were not introduced without friction. Some teachers had difficulty working with remedial teachers in their classroom, either because the remedial teachers seemed unsure of their role or because they tended to dominate the class, taking over from the class teacher. Even when an excellent working relationship was eventually established, this was only after a period of initial caution

Many questions about the introduction and possible extension of this scheme in other areas can, of course, be asked. One is whether English l.e.a.'s would in practice be able to give as decisive a lead as appears to have been the case in Scotland. In some l.e.a.'s with elaborate and long-established machinery for consultation between teachers and the l.e.a., the scheme might fall at the first fence. Its implicit direction in the organisation of provision for children with special needs might be seen as striking at the heart of the head teachers' autonomy.

The same argument could be levelled against the way the remedial specialists were distributed throughout schools. In Grampian, for example, they were based on 'pyramids' of secondary schools and their feeding primaries. This carries the possibility of friction between primary schools which could feel they are being compared with each other, perhaps compounded by a fear that the secondary school might seek to exert undue influence through the remedial teacher's activities. Yet it also carries the opportunity for improving co-operation both between primary and secondary schools, and between the primary schools themselves. No form of organisation is immune from criticism. The important point is that the administrative structure set up to meet the special needs of pupils in ordinary schools should not itself facilitate the identification of some children as failures. This objection would seem to be relevant in any proposal to establish special units in ordinary schools, through the parallel career structures and administrative support for teachers in ordinary and in special education.

School Based Development

Overview

Projects in individual schools and individual l.e.a.'s have already been mentioned in this book, and described in greater detail elsewhere (e.g. Booth and Statham, 1982; Booth and Potts, 1983; Galloway and Goodwin, 1979; Hegarty and Pocklington, 1981, 1982). Many of these reports are encouraging for their descriptions of good practice. It is clear that teachers, psychologists and administrators have successfully found ways to overcome the resistance and inertia of vested interests. It is clear, too, that raising the quality of education for children with special needs has benefited children and teachers throughout the school.

Yet the overall picture is far from rosy. Booth and Statham (1982) give disturbing accounts of children's and parents' experiences of special education. Contributors to Barton and Tomlinson's (1981) book suggest that much special educational provision exists to serve the interests of teachers in the mainstream rather than of children with special needs. This theme is developed by Ford *et al.* (1982) in their account of the 'invisible disasters' arising from the function of special education in removing troublesome pupils from the mainstream. It is also developed by Tomlinson (1981) in her penetrating account of the processes leading to placement in a school for ESN(M) pupils, and in her sociological critique of special education (Tomlinson, 1982).

Descriptions of 'invisible disasters' may give a one-sided picture. They undoubtedly serve to remind us, though, that stimulating accounts of apparently successful innovation may be equally one-sided. Moreover, the sociologist's contribution to the debate on special education has focused so far mainly on the role of separate special schools for the ESN(M) or the maladjusted in maintaining the existing social order in schools by removing the deviant pupils who fail to conform. As far as it goes, this argument is certainly valid. Its limitation lies in the fact that an administrative or legal decision to meet all special needs in ordinary schools, by abolishing special schools and transferring their resources, will not *per se* do anything to reduce the number of invisible disasters. As other sociologists have demonstrated, the experience of ordinary secondary schooling can be profoundly depressing for a large minority of pupils (e.g. Willis, 1977; Corrigan, 1979; Hargreaves, 1967, 1983).

Teaching children with special needs can be a source of great satisfaction, or a source of considerable stress. Without an adequate organisational structure, supported by adequate professional and material resources, the pupils can become a focus for their teachers' resentment. This can also happen when careful thought has been given to provision for the children concerned, and when adequate resources are available. It is most likely when staff morale is low, with a general air of resentment. No proposals for the organisation of provision for children with special needs can create a climate which ensures effective teaching and learning. Nevertheless, the way provision is organised can create its own problems. We need now to consider some of the possibilities and some of the pitfalls.

A Special Needs Department

A cynic might describe the most obvious response to the 1981 Education Act in secondary schools as a change in the remedial department's name to the special needs department. In primary schools the part-time remedial teacher becomes the part-time special needs teacher. It is still too early to say how far a change in name will in fact be reflected in a change in practice. Tomlinson's (1982) suggestion that the Act may increase the number of pupils following a separate, low-status curriculum deserves to be taken seriously. Several reasons may be put forward for this depressing possibility.

The Act legitimises the view that a large minority of pupils have special needs. It is a short step from here to concluding that:

(1) These pupils not only have problems, but are problems.
(2) Special needs require special provision.
(3) This requires modifications in the curriculum for pupils requiring this special provision.
(4) The special needs department should therefore set up its own classes to provide the modified curriculum 'needed' by the pupils concerned.

The most dangerous part of this argument is its hand-on-the-heart commitment to the interests of pupils with special needs, demonstrated by an eager readiness to allocate scarce teaching staff for the purpose. The effect, however, may be to reproduce all the worst characteristics of former remedial departments in the new special needs department. Worse, the number of pupils placed in the new departments may increase.

HMI will doubtless continue to draw attention to good practice and to criticise inconsistency in policy or inadequacy in practice when they visit schools. L.e.a.'s too will doubtless continue to encourage what they perceive as good practice. The Scottish HMI pre-empted the 1981 Act with its far-sighted critique of existing remedial provision, published in the same year as the Warnock Report (SED, 1978). A year later their colleagues in England and Wales noted that a majority of remedial teachers in secondary schools were part-time, with less than five years teaching experience (DES, 1979). In addition they criticised the restricted curriculum for less able pupils. Yet there is little evidence that HMI have any consistent policy towards academic organisation, such as ability banding, setting or streaming. Having accepted that a range of procedures involving selection by ability may be appropriate it becomes logically difficult for HMI to criticise a separate remedial department unless the department can be seen to be offering an unnecessarily restricted curriculum and to be staffed by under-qualified or inexperienced teachers.

Nor can much be expected from l.e.a. administration. At present administrative supervision, policy development and advisory support is hopelessly split between the traditional special school sector and the mainstream. In many l.e.a.'s, the chances of a unified approach to special needs seem little less remote now than before Warnock's Committee published its report.

It is important to be clear about the scope for extending the old hotch potch concept of remedial education into the new special needs departments, with all the associated implications of removal from the mainstream and a restricted curriculum. Integration into activities in the mainstream can be achieved through registration classes, extra-curricula activities and non-examined subjects such as PE or even art and craft. None of these seriously threaten the full-time nature of the remedial class, at least as far as the 'important' subjects in the mainstream curriculum are concerned. At the same time, the special needs department should, without too much difficulty, be able to make out a reasonable case that their programmes are based on assessment of individual pupils' needs. From their point of view, and from that of the school's management, the point is to demonstrate that special provision is based on the pupils' current needs.

The possibility that these needs may have been created by policy, attitudes and lack of provision in the mainstream may be a suitable topic for debate by academic sociologists and trendy educational psychologists. It need not, in practice, unduly worry head teachers who use their school's special needs department to increase the number of pupils in full-time, or nearly full-time separate provision. One hopes that these schools will find themselves in a minority. They will be conforming to the letter of the Act while ignoring its spirit. More seriously, they will be doing little or nothing to raise mainstream teachers' awareness of the needs of many of their pupils, nor to promote their confidence in working with them.

Withdrawal Groups

Most provision for children with special needs in primary schools is organised on the basis of part-time withdrawal from ordinary classes for extra, or 'remedial' help. This pattern is also prevalent in secondary schools. Some children have particular, possibly short-term, needs which can be met by a period of intensive learning in a small group or individually. Others have long-term needs which may be seen as requiring part-time provision throughout their school career. A teaching programme based on an assessment of each child's needs is a necessary starting point if part-time withdrawal from ordinary classes is to be effective. This has implications both for the selection of pupils and for the size of group.

At one level this becomes a logistical problem, concerned primarily with numbers. A junior school may be able to offer children in its top two year groups extra help with reading for four twenty-minute sessions weekly. If twelve pupils are thought to need extra help, one possibility is to give all twelve, four twenty-minute sessions. A second possibility is to give two groups of six, two twenty-minute sessions each. A third possibility is to spend three sessions with one group of six, and one session with the other group.

In theory, research should be able to tell us the best way to allocate resources. One question is whether children benefit more from intensive work in a very small group once or twice a week, compared with a larger group three or four times weekly. Another question is which children benefit most from which form of provision.

Sadly, in the real world research seldom provides tidy answers to complex questions. Even if it did, its usefulness would be severely limited by practical considerations. Clark (1979) argues that withdrawal sessions are too narrow and too specific, with little evidence that the skills acquired in the withdrawal group transfer to the regular class. In addition, whatever may happen in theory, in practice withdrawal groups are at the mercy of administrative expedience. This operates on at least four levels.

(1) If a teacher in a mainstream class is absent, the obvious replacement is the special needs teacher who 'only' has a small withdrawal group. Just as part-time special needs teachers are a prime target for cuts in the education budget, so their work is a prime target when someone is needed to fill in for an absent colleague.

(2) Withdrawal groups are necessarily time-tabled when teachers are available to take them. This can result in some disturbing anomalies. A pupil for whom art and music are the only real sources of satisfaction at school may find himself being removed from these lessons for extra help with maths, which he loathes. Only by rare coincidence is a pupil removed to receive extra help from the subjects in which he has been failing.

(3) A combination of time-table constraints and shortage of part-time teaching provision for children with special needs can ensure that notions about fitting a particular child into a particular group become fanciful. In reality, children have to be fitted in wherever there is a space. However generous the provision may be, the demand for it will always exceed supply.

(4) The fourth level at which withdrawal groups are at the mercy of administrative experience is perhaps the most damaging. The existence of provision for children with special needs in part-time classes may reduce the regular class or subject teachers' commitment to working with the pupils concerned themselves. Just as responsibility can be subtly transferred on to an educational psychologist, so it can be transferred to a remedial or special needs teacher. This is reflected in the extraordinary lack of liaison between many remedial teachers and their mainstream colleagues. In primary schools, where the remedial specialist is frequently part-time, this problem is widespread. In secondary schools, with their subject divisions and complex time-tables it becomes even more acute. Work carried out in withdrawal groups often seems to take place in glorious isolation from what is happening in the child's ordinary class.

In theory, this problem does not arise. Head teachers talk enthusiastically and frequently convincingly about the excellent liaison between teachers. Staffroom relationships may indeed be excellent, but this does not necessarily imply any kind of co-operation between mainstream teachers and their colleagues responsible for withdrawing pupils for extra help. Two reasons come to mind. First, teaching is an intensely private affair (Hargreaves, 1978). Joint planning involves exposing the strengths and the weaknesses in one's curriculum and teaching programme. This is potentially threatening, both for the class teacher and for the remedial specialists. 'Exercising my own professional judgement' about the child's needs can be an euphemism for 'doing my own thing'. The second reason is that mainstream teachers are often thankful that the child is being removed, if only for one or two periods. Co-operating in the remedial programme requires them to spend still more time on pupils who have already had more than their fair share.

Mixed Ability Teaching

The principle that children with special needs should be taught in ordinary mixed ability classes has implications both for professional support and for material resources. We also need to recognise that the examination system imposes its own constraints on the practical possibility of mixed-ability teaching in secondary schools. While all options may in theory be open to all pupils, selection by the pupils themselves will generally ensure an uneven ability distribution between the possible choices. Classics and, to a lesser extent, modern languages, for example, are unlikely to attract their fair share of non-examination candidates.

A further point is that commitment to mixed ability teaching is in no way incompatible with part-time withdrawal for special provision, or even with full-time withdrawal. The reason is that the special provision is seen not as an end in itself, but rather as a way of facilitating the pupil's return to mainstream mixed ability classes at the earliest opportunity. This aim implies that:

(1) No open-ended commitment to separate provision is entered into.
(2) The curriculum in the special classes is linked directly with that in ordinary classes.
(3) Both the special needs teachers and the regular class or

subject teachers accept that the pupils will be returning to ordinary classes, where the latter will have day-to-day responsibility for them.

Class teachers in primary schools and subject teachers in secondary schools cannot, however, reasonably be expected to accept responsibility for these children without appropriate support. There is little evidence of far-reaching changes in most l.e.a.'s since HMI's report drew attention to the limitations in much remedial teaching in England and Wales (DES, 1979). Asking inexperienced teachers to give their more experienced and full-time colleagues professional guidance on how to teach children with special needs is hardly a recipe for success. It follows that a policy of mixed ability teaching, with its implication that special needs should be met mainly in ordinary classes, requires generous provision of resources and experienced staff.

E. Jones (1983) advocates a flexible resource department as a way of catering for pupils' individual needs. She sees special education 'as a continuum of services radiating from the ordinary classroom' and suggests five roles for the department's teachers:

(1) To withdraw pupils for clearly defined reasons on an individual or group basis.
(2) To provide some pupils with an alternative to certain lessons.
(3) To work with colleagues in the mainstream, giving some pupils on-the-spot help and monitoring the work presented to the group as a whole.
(4) To act as consultants on particular pupils.
(5) To ensure that pupils receive the necessary time-table and equipment to enable them to remain with their peer group.

As described here, the notion of a resources department does not necessarily imply mixed ability teaching throughout the school. On the other hand, effective mixed ability teaching does imply the existence of a flexible resources department. Some schools will prefer to give the resources department a central base, visible and accessible to pupils and teachers alike. Others will argue that this emphasises the separate nature of special educational provision which the department should be seeking to avoid.

A secondary school in New Zealand, visited as part of a research programme on provision for disruptive pupils (Galloway and

Barrett, 1982), had a strikingly clear policy for its special education department. Pupils could be withdrawn on a part-time or full-time basis for short periods. Throughout the school, though, there was recognition that they would soon return to the mainstream, where they and their teachers would receive support from members of the special education department's network. Since teachers had been accustomed since the school opened to team work, and to seeing each other teach, the presence of a 'stranger' in the ordinary classroom presented no problem.

Provision of material resources to enhance each pupil's opportunity of success was considered central to the special education department's work. This did not involve a central resource bank, but rather the gradual establishment of department-based resources. Thus, subject specialists had direct access to resources suitable for their least able pupils. These resources might have been prepared in discussion with, and sometimes by, members of the special education network. Their base in the subject department helped to ensure that they were readily accessible. Equally important, it helped to create a climate in which subject teachers expected to accept responsibility for their pupils with special needs. In addition, competence in teaching the full ability range was seen by senior staff as central to their colleagues' professional development.

Conclusions

We have argued throughout this chapter that policy and provision for pupils with special needs requires a coherent philosophical underpinning both at l.e.a. level and at school level. No single approach provides a solution appropriate to all schools. Ferguson and Adams (1982) describe some of the tensions experienced by teachers in the Grampian team-teaching initiative in Scotland. E. Jones (1983), while advocating resource departments is frank about the practical problems when special resource teachers seek to accompany pupils into subject teacher's lessons, giving them on-the-spot help.

. . . too little advance information on lesson content, the didactic approach adopted by teachers in classrooms, which gave no role to special needs teachers other than listening, and in many instances de-skilled them since they did not know what to do when the subject teacher was absent or delayed. Frequently the resources staff had come to accept this undemanding role. (p. 145)

Such problems can, as Jones argues, be overcome. How far they are overcome, though, does not depend solely on the professional ability of the special needs staff, nor even on their success in establishing a co-operative relationship with their class teacher or subject teacher colleagues. It also depends heavily on the complex network of relationships between teachers, between pupils and between pupils and teachers which create the nebulous concept of school climate. One measure of school climate is the behaviour of pupils in and out of the classroom. Since pupils who present behaviour problems are regarded as often having special educational needs, it is necessary to consider ways in which some schools have responded to these needs.

5 RESPONSES TO DISTURBING BEHAVIOUR

Introduction

Criticisms may be levelled against the extended concept of special educational needs proposed by the Warnock Report and enshrined in the 1981 Education Act. These criticisms may apply with greatest force to the implication that children have special needs when teachers find their behaviour difficult. There may indeed be clear evidence that children's behaviour at school depends largely on the school and its teachers, leading to the conclusion that whether children show evidence, through their behaviour, of having special educational needs may depend mainly on the school rather than on factors in the children themselves or their families. It nevertheless remains the case that teachers in many schools do find the behaviour of a substantial minority of their pupils disturbing. The popularity of screening instruments such as Rutter's (1967) Behaviour Questionnaire or Scott's (1971) Bristol Social Adjustment Guides may depend less on their diagnostic usefulness than on their successfully identifying behavioural problems which are relatively prevalent, yet constitute real and legitimate sources of concern to teachers.

In this chapter we look briefly at some problems of definition, concluding that the categories most widely used by teachers and educational administrators are of little or no value in understanding the needs of the pupils concerned. Next we consider aspects of school organisation and the curriculum, asking how these may promote behaviour which is socially acceptable to teachers or provoke behaviour they consider socially unacceptable. We conclude that the evidence points to the need for a whole-school approach, with implications which affect all teachers and all pupils, not just an arbitrarily selected group with special needs. Finally we consider some responses to disturbing behaviour at l.e.a. level and within individual schools, concluding that most of these are at best of marginal value, since they are based on a false assessment of the problem.

The tone of this chapter is somewhat negative. This is unavoidable in discussing the red herrings that constitute the most frequent responses to behaviour problems. There is no cause, however, for despondency. Evidence accumulating over the last ten years shows that many behaviour problems can be prevented and that teachers can play an essential part in catering for those whose problems do still indicate that they require special attention. In the next two chapters we consider some of this evidence.

Spurious Categories

Disturbed or Disturbing?

When teachers or psychologists say that a child is disturbed they are making a value judgement about the child's behaviour. When they say that they find the behaviour disturbing, they are describing their own reaction. There is no objective quality in a child's behaviour which justifies a conclusion that a child is disturbed. To say so would be to infer an unspecified mental state from observed behaviour. This is acceptable, even necessary, when there is general agreement about the nature of the mental state. For example, we can conclude from someone's behaviour that he is happy or unhappy. No such consensus exists with respect to the quasi-medical concept of disturbance. Teachers, psychologists and psychiatrists use the term in different ways, with little idea what others mean by it, and frequently with only a hazy idea of what they mean by it themselves. The case of 10-year-old Joanne illustrates the argument.

Joanne had always been regarded as one of the class's slower pupils, but towards the middle of her penultimate junior school year her teacher started to complain to the head that her work was deteriorating still further. At the same time the teacher was becoming increasingly irritated by Joanne's behaviour, which she described as 'sulky', 'insolent' and 'couldn't care less'. Having taught the class himself in the teacher's absence the head recognised the descriptions. Unlike her colleague, though, she did not regard them as evidence of disturbance. She knew that Joanne was finding much of the work difficult. In addition her parents were academically ambitious and put considerable pressure on her to do better. The head was on the point of yielding to the class teacher's insistence that Joanne be referred to the school's psychologist when the teacher was taken ill, and was away for two months. The young supply teacher who took over the class had no complaints and no worries about Joanne's behaviour. Indeed he described her as one of the livelier members of the class, responsive to praise and encouragement. When the head looked at Joanne's work, it became clear that she had achieved more in the last two months than in the whole of the rest of the year.

Neither teachers nor psychologists will find anything surprising in this account. It does, however, indicate the logical and practical difficulties in saying that a child, or a child's behaviour, is disturbed. All that Joanne's class teacher could legitimately say was that *she* found her behaviour disturbing. The head teacher witnessed similar behaviour and did not find it disturbing. The young supply teacher elicited a different and much more constructive pattern of behaviour from Joanne, so the question whether she was disturbed or disturbing did not arise.

When teachers say that they find a child's behaviour disturbing, they are implying that the child is the focus of their concern, while acknowledging the significance of their own response to the child. The distinction between saying that children are disturbed and saying that they are disturbing is therefore not merely semantic. It brings us back to the question of responsibility discussed in the last chapter. As a teacher, if I say a child is disturbing I am accepting that the problem lies as much in my responses as in the behaviour itself. Hence, I retain some sense of responsibility for dealing with it. If I say that the child is disturbed I imply that the problem is someone else's, since as a teacher I am trained to teach and not to deal with 'disturbed' children.

Maladjusted or Disruptive?

The Warnock Report made no use of the term disturbed. Although the committee recommended abolishing the old categories of handicaps they retained the term maladjusted on the grounds that behaviour can meaningfully be considered only in relation to the circumstances in which it occurs. As Joanne's case indicates, this is true. Yet the objections to the term maladjusted are at least as strong as to the term disturbed. L.e.a.'s have special schools for maladjusted pupils. Thus if pupils are maladjusted they may be seen as someone else's responsibility.

Warnock's retention of the term maladjusted is not explicitly reflected in the 1981 Education Act, but since the number of special schools for maladjusted pupils and centres for disruptive ones shows no signs of decreasing this is a somewhat peripheral point. More important is the spurious distinction, rapidly becoming enshrined in DES folklore, between maladjusted and disruptive. In the 1970s centres and units for disruptive pupils gradually increased in popularity. An HMI survey (1978) showed that 72 per cent of 96 l.e.a.'s surveyed had established units by 1976. The number has increased since then. By 1983 more than 6,000 pupils were in so-called disruptive units (Newell, 1983), nearly as many as were in schools for the maladjusted. L.e.a.'s have generally been adamant that the units catered for disruptive, and not maladjusted pupils. In our work in Sheffield we regarded this as a cynical argument:

> Education officers gradually realised that it was usually cheaper and always administratively easier to open special centres for disruptive adolescents rather than expand the special school system . . . units were faced with fewer staffing constraints in the form of recommendations on pupil:teacher ratios in special schools (DES, 1973). They could be more flexible in their admission and discharge procedures. Pupils would always remain on the roll of their original school, to which it was theoretically hoped they would return. Having established these units l.e.a.s found themselves forced to deny that they catered for maladjusted children, since maladjusted children must — under the 1944 Act — be educated in special schools or classes for the maladjusted. (Galloway *et al.*, 1982*a*, p. 60)

It is not at all clear how far the 1981 Act has changed the situation. Pupils cannot normally be transferred to special schools on the grounds of maladjustment without the 'protection' of a Statement based on a formal assessment. On the other hand the DES (1983) has advised that formal procedures:

> are not required when ordinary schools provide special educational provision from their own resources in the form of additional tuition and remedial provision or, in normal circumstances, where the child attends a reading centre or unit for disruptive pupils (paragraph 15).

The DES guidelines are extraordinary for at least two reasons. First, the majority of centres for disruptive pupils are 'terminal' in the sense that few pupils are expected to return to the mainstream. Second, *all* pupils sent to units for the disruptive could equally well have been described as maladjusted if it could have served any useful administrative purpose. Their behaviour, according to teachers, is at least as disturbing as that of maladjusted pupils. The same applies to their family backgrounds. Whether a child is labelled disruptive or maladjusted has nothing to do with educational, psychological or medical assessment. It depends solely on the type of provision available locally.

Pupils not Categories

The muddle which, in different ways, both Warnock and the DES got themselves into over the usefulness of terms like maladjusted and disruptive should not be allowed to obscure three points. First, pupil's behaviour at school is strongly influenced by their experiences at school. The evidence shows that schools vary widely in their 'production' of pupils with behavioural problems, and that these differences are not attributable to catchment area factors. Second, pupils who present behaviour problems are regarded in terms of Warnock's report and of the 1981 Act as having special educational need. Since, however, their needs may to a large extent have arisen from their experiences at school it seems logical that responses should be based on analysis of the school's contribution as well as of the pupil. Third, Warnock's insistence on the extended concept of special needs is both legitimate and useful to the extent that it acknowledges that teachers are disturbed by the behaviour of a substantial minority of their pupils.

A further point, implicit in the discussion so far, is that there are no satisfactory criteria for distinguished between groups of pupils who disturb, nor for distinguishing between those whose needs can be met in an ordinary school and those requiring separate special education. In the great majority of cases, children are referred to special schools for the maladjusted or centres for the disruptive when teachers and educational psychologists decide that the ordinary school cannot or should not be expected to contain them any longer. Their decision may be influenced by pressure from the pupil's class teacher or by the view that the child needs to be removed for the benefit of other pupils. The decision is rationalised, though, as being in the child's best interests. We should therefore consider briefly whether there is in fact much evidence for the view that pupils benefit from transfer to separate provision.

The Case Against Separate Provision

On common-sense grounds it might seem surprising if pupils improved following transfer to special schools or centres. All teachers and all parents know that children learn from each other. One wonders what they are supposed to learn when placed in a separate school or class with a lot of other pupils presenting similarly severe behaviour problems. In this connection it is irrelevant whether the special provision is a class operated as part of the school's special education network, or a separate school or centre serving the whole l.e.a.

The limited available evidence on the progress of pupils in special schools for maladjusted or delinquent pupils is reviewed elsewhere (Galloway and Goodwin, 1979). The evidence does *not* suggest that these schools are frequently successful in returning pupils to the mainstream, nor that placement results in any long-term improvement in the pupil's behaviour. The most plausible conclusion is that the behaviour of pupils, like that of adults, changes according to the circumstances. In other words, disturbing behaviour must be investigated and tackled in the context in which it occurs. Seen in this light, the failure of attempts to tackle the problem out of context meet with predictable failure, (*see* Clarke and Cornish, 1978). Even when the aim of special centres for disruptive pupils is successful entry to employment rather than return to school, there is little evidence that this is frequently achieved (e.g. Galloway and Barrett, 1984).

The evidence, then, does not suggest that pupils' special needs are well served by removal from ordinary schools. In one sense, the debate is of peripheral importance. However extensive an l.e.a.'s provision for maladjusted or disruptive pupils may be, separate schools or centres will never cater for more than a tiny minority of the pupils whose teachers find aspects of their behaviour disturbing or troublesome. We return, therefore, to the school environment.

The Curriculum and School Organisation

Overview

A conventional topic on in-service courses for teachers is what can be done about disruptive pupils. The trouble is not so much that the question is unanswerable as that it is based on the premise that something needs to be done to, or for, the pupils. Their behaviour may well suggest that they have special needs but their needs are intricately bound up with those of their teachers. The question can be re-worded to ask what experiences pupils derive from school which facilitate behaviour that teachers find disturbing.

This question does not only apply to anti-social and disruptive pupils. It applies equally to timid, shy or withdrawn pupils who can seldom be persuaded to take part in classroom activities and appear isolated or even socially ostracised in the playground. It is sometimes argued that if teachers were not so busy dealing with disruptive behaviour they could become more aware of the needs of children with equally severe emotional problems who are not outwardly disruptive.

There is anecdotal evidence for this. Educational psychologists sometimes find that they receive more referrals of children with emotional or specific psychological problems, for example phobias or stammering, from schools in which disruptive behaviour is regarded as a relatively minor problem. In schools where disruptive behaviour is the dominant problem for teachers, it also accounts for the bulk of referrals to psychologists. There is not, however, much research evidence for this view. If low rates of disruptive behaviour enable teachers to recognise other more 'emotional' problems, we would expect the latter to be relatively more prevalent in schools with low rates of disruptive behaviour than in schools with high rates.

So far research has not confirmed this prediction. A more plausible prediction is that schools which have successfully reduced or eliminated the problem of disruptive behaviour will also reduce the prevalence of problems which cause more distress to the pupils themselves than to their teachers. The needs of socially isolated pupils will perhaps be more readily recognised if disruptive behaviour presents relatively little problem. On the other hand, if classroom relationships between teachers and pupils are generally co-operative, shy or anxious pupils may have greater confidence to participate, and hence may give less evidence of having special needs in the first place.

Asking how pupils' experiences at school affect their behaviour demands a multivariate reply. We can accept that the way a person responds to particular experiences will depend on the individual's temperament and previous experiences. In the past, though, this had led to excessive focus on the individual's response, with corresponding neglect to the potentially damaging experiences at school which provoke the responses.

The Curriculum

An immense amount of work has been carried out in the last 30 years on curriculum development. A disproportionate amount of this effort has been spent on designing new curricula for less able pupils. This has had the unfortunate side-effect of creating two curricula, one high status and the other low status. Whatever some teachers may believe, pupils are seldom in any doubt about the purpose of community studies, voluntary service in the community and a range of work experience projects. As Hargreaves (1983) points out, the pupils on these programmes *and* pupils in examination classes see their aims as freeing teachers to devote more time and attention to the latter. The message conveyed to both groups through the hidden curriculum, David Hargreaves concludes, is disastrous.

Hargreaves' call is for a radical re-thinking of the secondary curriculum. He not only regards the existing secondary school curriculum as divisive, but thinks that both its structure and content disadvantage working class pupils. He chaired a committee for the Inner London Education Authority on underachievement in comprehensive schools. The report (ILEA, 1984) argued that the traditional course leading to 'O' level or to the Certificate in Secondary Education provided a 'vague two year educational journey leading to distant and nebulous goals'. Instead the committee believed that the curriculum should be re-organised on a system of six to eight week learning units, each of which would have a 'more readily defined and perceived purpose, content and method of recording'.

Within the recommended 11 or 12 inter-connected units comprising the pupils' last two years at school, compulsory areas would be an arts subject, personal and social education, craft design and technology, and science. This involves extending the concept of a common curriculum. While acknowledging that some degree of choice for pupils in the final two years of compulsory schooling is desirable, the Hargreaves committee thought that a common curriculum should account for 60 – 70 per cent of the time-table. The report discussed as 'often merely an excuse for poor teaching' the view that disaffection often results from lack of subject choice.

The Hargreaves committee was concerned with underachievement in secondary schools, not specifically with special educational needs. Yet the extended concept of special educational needs envisaged by the 1981 Act is inextricably tied up with ill-defined concepts such as underachievement and disaffection. By definition, pupils who are significantly underachieving, and whose disaffection present problems to their teachers, are assumed to have special educational needs according to both the Warnock Report and to the 1981 Act. The value of Hargreaves' work is:

(1) Its focus on the importance of the curriculum as a whole.
(2) The argument that both its content and its structure stand in urgent need of review.
(3) Its emphasis on the needs of pupils throughout the school, not simply on the least able or most severely problematic minority.
(4) Its emphasis on the relationships between the curriculum, underachievement and pupil disaffection.

These issues are not, needless to say, confined to secondary schools, though it is in the last two years of compulsory education that the problems of underachievement and disruptive behaviour have received most attention. Moreover, however desirable reforms such as those advocated by the Hargreaves committee may be, school effectiveness will still depend largely on other factors. Rutter's (1979) study of London schools was published four years before the ILEA report, and described schools apparently varying widely in their pupils' behaviour and progress. This does not decry the usefulness of wide-ranging reviews which reappraise existing policy and have implications for all schools. It merely underlines the facts:

(1) That no amount of development or reappraisal is likely to reduce inequality within schools nor to reduce the differences between schools.
(2) That a great deal can be done within the constraints of existing policies and resources.

The possibility, and potential, of reviewing existing practice directs attention to teaching process rather than the currriculum content. At its simplest, the question is what opportunities the school provides for success. Re-phrasing the question:

(1) How far does the curriculum enhance pupils' self-esteem?
(2) Do they derive a sense of developing competence from their
    activities in the formal curriculum?

These questions are independent of the pupils' age and of curriculum content. They relate to the opportunities for success and for
failure which exist in the curriculum. They also relate to the way
schools respond to failure or to disturbing behaviour. The pupil's
failure can be seen as evidence that the teacher's methods, materials
and objectives need reviewing. This does not imply failure or inadequacy on the teacher's part, but rather a professional willingness to
learn from the pupil's performance. Another pattern is for the
pupil's failure to be seen as the *pupil's* problem, requiring part-time
or full-time withdrawal for special or remedial help.

The relationship between lack of progress in the curriculum, self-
image and disturbing behaviour cannot easily be overstated. Pupils
who recognise that they are making progress in their classroom
work, and who know that their progress is recognised and appre-
ciated by their teachers, and preferably also by their parents,
seldom present behavioural problems. The special education
department in one New Zealand school went a stage further.
Disruptive or otherwise disturbing behaviour in the classroom was
seen as evidence that the pupil's needs were not adequately being
met. In this context it did not matter greatly whether the pupil was
disruptive, anxious or socially isolated. The emphasis was on
enhancing self-image through success in the curriculum. The fact
that the curriculum might need modification in the light of the
pupils' needs was acknowledged as part of the teacher's job, aided
when necessary by members of the special education network
(Galloway and Barrett, 1982).

In this sense the sociologists' view that schools inevitably
reproduce the divisions within society is not so much wrong as one-
sided. No-one has yet suggested how schools can reduce inequality.
Nor has anyone suggested how they can avoid reproducing many of
the divisions that exist in society. That, however, does not imply
anything about the experiences they provide their pupils. For the
minority of pupils leaving school without the basic literacy skills,
they may have provided seemingly interminable experience of
frustration. The anti-school 'counter-culture' evident in some, but
not all, secondary schools may be seen as the pupils' response to a
feeling that their achievements are not valued. Feeling that they

have little scope for contributing anything useful on the school's terms, they derive a sense of belonging from membership of the counter-culture rather than from membership of the school itself. Failing to win social approval through the curriculum and the school's formal activities they obtain it in other ways.

This does not mean that the curriculum is the only factor affecting pupils' experiences at school. Since the curriculum constitutes the school's raison d'etre, however, it should be the starting point for any assessment of the special needs of pupils whose behaviour disturbs their teachers. The success of the most imaginative curriculum, though, depends partly on relatively mundane aspects of school organisation.

Time-tabling

The ways in which the time-table creates a source of confusion and tension for pupils and for teachers are not always recognised. Rabinowitz (1981) illustrates two of the problems. Schools, he argues can:

> . . . resemble large, and not very well organised, factories. In a factory of, say, 2,000 workers (pupils), 100 charge-hands (teachers), 20 foremen (senior staff) and 2 or 3 directors (head and deputies), it would be astonishing to find a work force that would accept a system in which each worker was engaged on 7 or 8 different pieces of work each day, for several different charge-hands in 7 or 8 different work places, to 7 or 8 different standards. This, effectively, is what occurs in many secondary schools under conditions which often would not meet accepted trade union requirements (pp. 82 – 3).

The complexity of the secondary school time-table is not the only source of tension, though. Frequently the complexity is compounded by the juxtaposition of certain subjects and even by the physical constraints of the school's buildings. Rabinowitz comments:

> In many schools children are expected to cover quite large distances in what almost amounts to negative time. One lesson begins at 10 a.m., for example, while the other ends at 10 a.m., but little allowance is made for pupils who arrive 'late'. And the teacher who arrives late for the same reason may start off with a

disruptive class who have been kept waiting. Different kinds of lesson activities can interact with each other. Physical education is often found to precede lessons in which there is a high incidence of problem behaviour. The reason for this is not just that children find it difficult to accept ordinary classroom constraints after the freedom of physical expression, but also that PE teachers are often more likely than other staff to be able to 'put down' pupils who are troublesome. Any resentment of this may be vented on the next teacher, particularly if he is young and inexperienced, the lesson unpopular and towards the end of a tiring day. (p. 83)

Rabinowitz's example illustrates how discussion of children's special educational needs is largely meaningless unless considered in the context in which these needs are expressed. To the extent that an over-loaded, over complex or inadequately planned time-table facilitates disruptive behaviour it makes effective teaching more difficult. Anything which increases the opportunities for boredom or failure in the curriculum creates fertile conditions for problems which later can be taken as evidence of a pupil having special educational need.

Diffused Responsibilities

Every pupil should feel that at least one teacher in the school takes a particular interest in him or her as an individual and in his or her general progress. One of the aims of pastoral care is to provide this sense of caring. Purely from an administrative point of view, the person with basic responsibility for pastoral care must be the class teacher in primary schools and the form tutor in secondary schools. The head and deputy cannot hope to take effective responsibility for pupils' pastoral care, at least in medium sized or larger primary schools, nor can the year tutor or head of house hope to do so in secondary schools. This does not, of course, imply that senior staff have no pastoral responsibilities, but rather that their responsibility is to promote the pastoral care activities of their colleagues (*see* Chapter 7). Special needs can be recognised at an early stage by teachers involved in day-to-day work with the pupil. In practice, though, responsibility is frequently so diffused that early signs of stress, reflected in the pupil's behaviour or progress, go unrecognised because they are not recognised as any one teacher's responsibility.

The role of secondary school form tutors provides a good example. In two research programmes involving 14 schools in Sheffield and New Zealand, we found consensus amongst head teachers that class or form tutors were the basic unit of pastoral care. In practice, though, form tutors appeared to play an active part in pastoral care at relatively few schools. Galloway (1983) suggested five factors which could combine to reduce the form tutor's effectiveness:

(1) Class tutors changed every year.
(2) Class tutors seldom taught pupils in their tutor group.
(3) Class tutors only saw their tutor group for ten minutes once or twice daily, and had to spend virtually all this time on administrative chores, such as completing attendance registers.
(4) Class tutors felt that year tutors were paid to do pastoral care, and saw no reason for accepting the responsibility themselves.
(5) The year tutor's job was defined in terms of investigating and dealing with problems, rather than as leader of a pastoral team.

In primary schools where one teacher normally has responsibility for the same class for all or most of the week the teacher's pastoral responsibility should be more straightforward. In practice this is not always the case. Pastoral care in primary schools has attracted remarkably little attention in its own right. It is almost as though the schools' pastoral function is taken for granted in primary schools, becoming a matter for debate only on transfer to the larger and potentially, though not necessarily, impersonal secondary school. Yet the scope of primary school class teachers can be restricted by aspects of the school's organisation in similar ways to that of secondary form tutors. In each case the result is the same, namely to restrict the professional development of teachers and to impose a limitation on their work with all their pupils, particularly those who may develop special educational needs.

In practice, this can happen in four ways in primary schools:

(1) The head centres pastoral care on herself and/or the deputy, insisting on holding all discussions with educational welfare officers, educational psychologists, social workers and other 'outsiders' herself. Some headteachers rationalise this as 'protecting'

their colleagues. The effect is to devalue class teachers' knowledge of the pupils and to reduce its potential usefulness by filtering it through a third party.

(2) Assembly involving the whole school is held daily, with class teachers being encouraged to deal with administrative chores such as registration in the first five minutes of the morning and afternoon. As a result the class has little or no time allocated for activities which are not seen as part of the formal curriculum. As a result, teachers who in theory pride themselves on teaching the whole child — 'children not subjects' — in practice define educational activities in unnecessarily limited terms.

(3) The head insists on parents not approaching class teachers direct to discuss their children's progress. Again, this is rationalised as 'protecting' class teachers. Yet in practice, this too devalues the class teacher's knowledge. Occasionally heads who are happy to allow class teachers to discuss their children's progress with parents draw the line at discussion of behaviour problems, except at a superficial level on the annual open evening. Again the spurious distinction implicitly conveyed to class teachers is that their responsibility lies in the area of educational development rather than social/emotional development.

(4) The head encourages class teachers to 'play down' concern about a pupil's behaviour, either on the grounds that 'we can cope with him for the time being', or that 'it's not really too much of a problem yet', or that 'he'll grow out of it', or that 'we mustn't expect too much: just look at the home background'. Thus class teachers may recognise special needs, but be encouraged to ignore them on the assumption that time, the great healer, will work its own cure without intervention or help from teachers.

Deliberately, these points parody the concern of many primary schools for their pupils. In many primary schools, class teachers are not only expected to take wider pastoral responsibilities, but given every opportunity to do so by the head and senior staff. No adviser or educational psychologist with much experience in primary schools, though, will be unfamiliar with the examples given above. As in secondary schools, these are aspects of organisation and of administrative style which can provide fertile ground for minor problems to develop into bigger ones.

This is also seen both in primary and in secondary schools in the diffusion of responsibility for dealing with discipline problems.

Both Lawrence *et al.* (1977) and Galloway *et al.* (1982*a*) have noted how relatively minor problems can escalate into major confrontations. Instead of helping class or subject teacher colleagues deal with an incident themselves, senior staff sometimes accept the problem as their own responsibility. This removes the incident from a matter between pupil and teacher to a matter between pupil and the school's hierarchy. In such circumstances it becomes fatally easy for either side to take up an entrenched position from which retreat becomes impossible.

This is a frequent pattern in suspensions from secondary schools, and is by no means unknown in confrontations in primary schools, especially when parents become involved. Rather than advise the class teacher on ways to de-escalate the situation, the head feels that she must take personal responsibility for supporting her colleague. The parents, sensing the tension both from the head's manner and from the fact that they are dealing with the head rather than with the class teacher react defensively. In these circumstances the problem is more often shelved than solved, allowing an undercurrent of resentment or suspicion to cloud future relationships.

We are not arguing that class teachers should be expected to deal personally with all problems that arise, and certainly not that they should be expected to so so unaided by senior staff. On the other hand we are arguing that no teacher can shelve responsibility for pupils' development, including those aspects of psycho-social development which are reflected in their behaviour. For practical purposes, this means that responsibility starts with the class teacher in a primary school and the form tutor in a secondary. Their effectiveness, though, will depend to some extent on the support available from the l.e.a. (*see* pp. 62 – 7) and within the school.

Provision Within the School

Underlying Assumptions

The major problem with l.e.a. responses to disturbing behaviour is that the parallel 'special' system reduces the scope and effectiveness of support that can be offered to ordinary schools. The 'hidden agenda' of possible special school referral acts as a powerful constraint. An even more difficult problem facing 'outsiders' is that the child's special needs are identified in the ordinary class, and may be created by factors within the class. They can also be dealt with there. Yet whatever may happen in theory, in practice teachers seldom accept advice unless the advice-givers have established their credibility. This is not easy for educational psychologists responsible for visiting up to thirty schools. Responsibility, therefore, must start with head-teachers and their staff.

In considering how to respond to the special needs of their disturbing pupils, a useful starting point is with two underlying assumptions:

(1) The peer group is potentially the strongest pro-social and supportive influence in the school. It is also, potentially, the most anti-social and destructive influence.

(2) Experience of success in a well balanced curriculum is potentially the most valuable means available to teachers in enhancing pupils' self-esteem, and hence of helping the school to achieve its aims. Conversely, repeated experience of frustration and failure will have the reverse effect.

How are these assumptions reflected in the special classes and units for disruptive pupils which have achieved such popularity over the last five to ten years?

On-site Units

The early on-site units were based in primary schools in West Sussex, constituting an attempt to provide help for maladjusted children in ordinary schools (Labon, 1973). Teachers in the groups were appointed by the head, but worked closely with the authority's educational psychologists. The aims were explicitly therapeutic, with an emphasis on creative activities which promoted co-operative relationships. At about the same time the Inner London Education Authority was establishing 'nurture' groups in infant schools to cater for children, mostly from socially disadvantaged backgrounds, who presented serious behavioural problems at school (Boxall, 1973; Gorrell-Barnes, 1973). In the secondary sector N. Jones (1973, 1974) described a project at Brislington Comprehensive school in Bristol. This too was seen as a way of using the skills of the school's educational psychologist to help teachers run a therapeutic group for maladjusted pupils.

Evaluation of the West Sussex groups suggested that up to two-thirds of pupils improved in their relationships with other children and with adults, but that the children least likely to benefit were those whose behaviour was most overtly disruptive (Labon, 1974; Archer, 1973). In America Vacc (1968) noted improvement whilst the children attended a special group, but found this was not maintained on return to ordinary lessons (Vacc, 1972).

It is not clear how far these early groups encouraged the huge increase in on-site provision for disturbing pupils in the second half of the 1970s, and in the 1980s. It seems probable that suggestions by individual educational psychologists were instrumental in establishing the first units, but that the idea was then taken up and developed by head teachers and by administrators who saw it as a tidy solution to the problem of problem children. There has certainly been 'widespread concern that special groups may function as "sin-bins" whose function is simply to contain trouble makers' (Galloway *et al.*, 1982a).

As with off-site units, there is a lack of research both on how the groups operate, and on their usefulness. In a detailed study of seven groups in Sheffield secondary schools we found an astonishingly favourable pupil:teacher ratio, ranging from 1.6:1, to 5.3:1. This is more favourable than would be found in any special school. One might expect, then, that the groups would be able to cater in a very specialised and intensive way for the pupils' needs. This was not, however, the general picture.

The curriculum tended to be much narrower than that followed by pupils in the mainstream. Moreover, except in one group there appeared to be little attempt to link the curriculum followed by the pupil's ordinary class with the curriculum followed by the group. Subject teachers were usually reluctant to accept the extra work entailed in providing suitable work for pupils to complete while attending the group. In consequence, it was hardly surprising that some pupils had difficulty picking up the threads when they returned to ordinary lessons. The extent to which the curriculum was based on an assessment of each pupil's individual needs varied from group to group. In general, though, there was little evidence of pupils following individually designed remedial programmes.

An argument frequently put forward in favour of special groups is that they help to prevent the need for suspension. At least in Sheffield, this was not the case. If anything the number of pupils suspended for disciplinary reasons in the first two years of the groups' existence was larger than the number suspended in the two years before the groups opened. We concluded:

With hindsight, one can see a depressing inevitability in some pupils' progress. Having frequently been in trouble in the main body of the school, they were referred to the group; on return from the group they found teachers expecting further trouble because they had been in the group; further confrontation occurred, culminating in the ultimate accolade of suspension (p. 130).

The usefulness of special groups in helping schools to contain their most disruptive pupils seems, therefore, to remain very much in question. It would be surprising if this were not the case. They are based on a false premise, namely that disturbing behaviour which occurs in one context can successfully be treated in another. Even if the pupil's behaviour improved dramatically while attending a special group, there is no reason to suppose that this improvement will be maintained on return to the classes in which the original problems occurred. Hence, we must also consider procedures which have aimed to help pupils and their teachers in the ordinary classroom setting.

Conclusions

Following a recent in-service course on responses to disruptive behaviour a representative from the l.e.a.'s administration admitted privately the real reason for opening an off-site centre for disruptive pupils. The real reason, he explained, had been to maintain morale amongst head teachers. Most of the local heads wanted the centre, seeing it as a necessary addition to the separate special education network in view of the probable phasing out of corporal punishment. The assistant education officer had done his arithmetic, and recognised that the proposed centre would be able to admit no more than one or two pupils annually from each school. Further, he recognised that very few classroom teachers would feel any benefit. Pupils would be referred because *senior* staff found them unmanageable; a majority of teachers in each school would never have come across the pupils in question, let alone have had problems teaching them. Clearly, the demand came from heads and deputy heads.

This education officer's impression was consistent with the reception which Sheffield's first centre for disruptive pupils

received. With some notable exceptions, senior staff were enthusiastic. At least one educational psychologist was even handed a
long list of candidates. He pointed out that if the school received its
fair share of places, in proportion to the l.e.a.'s total secondary
school role, one pupil would be admitted every two years. The
curious thing was that, in their enthusiasm for centres to which
disruptive pupils could be sent, many senior and experienced
teachers had failed to recognise how irrelevant they were to the day-
to-day problems of their colleagues.

Even when a special group is established by one school, serving
only that school's pupils, it is unlikely to provide a useful service to
many teachers in the school. In our study of seven such groups in
Sheffield we asked teachers whether a pupil had ever been removed
from a class they taught in order to attend the group (Galloway *et
al.*, 1982*a*). In the seven schools this was true of between 41 per cent
and 80 per cent of the teachers interviewed. More important, the
proportion of teachers who thought that *teachers* benefited from
the pupil's transfer ranged from 1 – 64 per cent. Further question-
ing revealed that even when a pupil had been removed from a
teacher's class, this was relatively seldom because the teacher we
were interviewing had experienced great difficulty with the pupil.

In a thought-provoking article, Lloyd-Smith (1979) argued that a
unit for disruptive pupils may reduce teachers' commitment to
dealing with problems themselves. When schools create specialists
to deal with children with problems, it becomes easier for class and
subject teachers to transfer responsibility from themselves on to the
specialists. Lloyd-Smith did not see the expansion of special provision for disruptive pupils as a response to changing patterns of
behaviour amongst pupils. Rather it reflected an ideological belief
amongst teachers and administrators that disruptive behaviour
should be investigated and dealt with by specialists.

The problem with this view, of course, is that schools vary widely
in the behaviour they regard as disruptive. The number of pupils
whose behaviour is sufficiently disturbing to justify a claim that
they have special needs also varies widely from school to school.
Since there is ample evidence that these differences between schools
cannot be attributed to catchment area factors we must look more
closely at the ways in which different schools cater for their pupils.
In particular we need to look at the effects, intended or otherwise,
of particular policies on *pupils'* perceptions of their life at school.
This will start to show why some innovations, such as behavioural

units, have had limited success. It will also show that they may nevertheless play a valuable part in a school's network of services for pupils with special needs. This, however, is only likely:

(1) When the special needs network operates as an integral aspect of a school's policy for all its pupils and
(2) When the school's policy is successfully reflected in day-to-day practice.

6 THE HIDDEN CURRICULUM, THE GUIDANCE NETWORK AND PROVISION FOR SPECIAL NEEDS

Introduction

A recurring theme throughout previous chapters has been that provision for children with special needs has implications for the curriculum offered to all children in the school. The traditional streaming system with an 'A' stream at the top and a remedial class at the bottom did not just enable selected children to have full-time remedial education. It affected both content and teaching method in the 'A' stream classes as well.

Yet the 'lessons' which children learnt at school extend far beyond what is taught in the classroom as the school's formal curriculum. At one school children learn, from experience, that the main function of a remedial class is to give the bright kids a chance. They learn that doing the minimum amount of work, scrawling graffiti on walls, interrupting the teacher, missing lessons, or not wearing correct uniform can all bring social approval from peers. In other schools serving similar catchment areas this sort of behaviour is rare precisely because the majority of pupils discourage it.

The Meaning of Failure

We suggested earlier that two of the most fundamental aims for any school might be to enhance pupils' self-concept, and to promote a feeling of developing competence. Pupils with special needs frequently have a low self-concept. This can be related to a feeling that their efforts and achievements are not valued. It can also be related to a feeling that they are not acquiring new skills, relevant to their immediate interests and future needs. If these pupils see academically more able pupils deriving personal satisfaction from school activities, receiving approval from teachers and parents, they will necessarily find ways to protect themselves from their sense of failure.

Failure, though, is not necessarily destructive. It becomes destructive only when the individual sees it as an indication of

115

personal inadequacy: 'I have failed because there is something wrong with me which I can't do anything about'. Seligman (1975) has argued that depression in adults may be seen as a response to a feeling of 'learned helplessness'. Treatment lies in showing the patient how he can regain control over his environment.

This concept has been extended to explain the behaviour of children with learning difficulties. Children who see themselves as 'dim' members of the 'thick class' are implicitly putting responsibility for their lack of progress on themselves. The cumulative deterioration in the work and behaviour of so many pupils with special needs as they progress through secondary school may then be seen as a denial of their ability to do anything about a personal attribute. The resulting apathy is at the same time self-protective ('it's not my fault') and self-destructive.

Yet this cumulative deterioration with its accompanying apathy is not inevitable. Nor is it linked to the pupils' own intellectual ability. It seems likely that learned helplessness results from children comparing themselves unfavourably with other pupils. From the pupils' perspective the purpose of school activities may too often be to compare them with each other. Teachers may think they are concerned with 'mastery training', emphasising competence for its own sake, but this is seldom the message received by children. In an important study Dweck (1977) claimed that children who are 'mastery oriented' do not see failure as evidence of personal inadequacy. Rather they see it as giving them information which they can use to modify, and hence improve specific aspects of their performance. Dweck argued that children should be taught, consciously, to use criticism constructively to improve future performance. Further, the ability to use criticism is more effective in helping pupils to cope with failure than success in previous activities.

Some pupils with special needs also protect themselves from failure by rejecting the school's values, relying for social support on membership of an anti-authority sub-culture. This is not inconsistent with the notion of learned helplessness. Indeed, some pupils may reject the school's values precisely because they feel they lack the personal attributes which will enable them to raise their performance in the tasks set by teachers. In this sense, membership of a disruptive, disaffected sub-culture may be a healthier response than the more generalised apathy which characterises the behaviour in school of some pupils with special needs.

The Hidden Curriculum

Yet disaffection from school is in no way inevitable. Just as the peer group can provide powerful inducements to disruptive behaviour, so it can provide an equally powerfully pro-social bias. One measure of a school's effectiveness may be the prevalence of apathetic or consciously disruptive behaviour amongst pupils with special needs. Another way of expressing this is that school effectiveness may reflect the messages conveyed through the school's climate, and the hidden curriculum.

The hidden curriculum is a widely and often loosely used term. We use it here to refer to relationships between pupils and teachers, between pupils, and between teachers which determine what pupils and teachers expect of each other and how they perceive each other. Most of the literature on the hidden curriculum emphasises its destructive, negative messages. This is legitimate, since teachers must clearly be concerned about messages conveyed to pupils through the hidden curriculum which are in opposition to what they are trying to achieve. The messages conveyed through the hidden curriculum are not, however, necessarily negative. The hidden curriculum reflects the overall climate of the school, which is determined by policy and practice in all aspects of the school's work.

In this chapter we discuss the relationships between a school's policy on ability grouping and messages which may be conveyed through the hidden curriculum. We then look briefly at the importance of other aspects of school organisation, arguing that these may provide sources of frustration to pupils and teachers alike. Finally we consider three approaches to pupil guidance in schools and discuss their implications for children with special needs.

Ability Grouping

With minor variations, secondary schools in Britain follow one of four policies on ability grouping (Wilcox and Eustace, 1980):

(1) Streaming, when each class in an annual intake is arranged hierarchichally, from the brightest to the dullest, and pupils remain with their class for all subjects until the option system requires them to specialise; even then, all classes taking any

one option are grouped according to ability.
(2) Setting: this is a variation on streaming, but classes are grouped by ability for particular subjects, for example maths or science.
(3) Banding: here pupils are divided into two, or less frequently three ability bands, but within each band each class is of mixed ability.
(4) Mixed ability: here teachers seek to ensure that every class contains pupils with the full range of intellectual ability and social backgrounds.

The most frequent variation is for certain subjects to be taught in banded or mixed ability groups, for example English, social studies, PE, art and music, whilst others are setted.

The policy in each school will obviously affect all pupils and all teachers. Its effect on some pupils may, however, be more beneficial, or harmful, than on others. The first question concerning us here is what informal messages pupils may receive, particularly pupils with special needs, from the formal organisation. The second question is whether the messages are inevitable given the constraints of an existing policy.

In his classic study of a secondary modern school, Hargreaves (1967) concluded that formation of a 'delinquent' subculture was made almost inevitable by the school's streaming policy. Pupils had been told ever since they entered the school that success in public examinations was the goal to which they should aspire. In their final two years of compulsory schooling, low stream pupils discovered that they would not be entered for public examinations. Having been 'written off' as examination prospects, it was as though they then 'wrote off' the school. Hargreaves showed that the delinquescent subculture affected not only the pupil's attitudes and progress in class, but also their activities outside the classroom. Low stream pupils, for example, were much less likely to take part in extra-curricular activities than pupils in higher streams.

There is clearly nothing inherent in a comprehensive school which will overcome this sort of problem, since comprehensives can also stream their pupils by ability. Indeed, an early study by Ford (1969) suggested that comprehensive schools were no more likely to promote equality of opportunityand mixing across social class divisions than schools in the old tripartite system. Arguments in favour of comprehensive schools, Ford maintained, were based on the false belief that early division into ability-based groups would be less likely in the comprehensive sytem. For the present discussion, though, the more important question is whether mixed ability grouping may give pupils a more constructive alternative to the cohesive, anti-school subculture often found in lower ability classes.

The evidence is remarkably limited. In a replication of Ford's study, Cohen and Fisher (1973) found more mixing across social classes in a comprehensive than in the schools in the tripartite system. The comprehensive they studied taught pupils in mixed ability groups until the start of the fourth year, whereas Ford's was streamed. Other studies have also suggested that mixed ability teaching results in social benefits (e.g. Clunies-Ross and Reid, 1980). In contrast, Willis (1977) believed that alienation from school was independent of the school's policy on ability grouping.

Evidence on the effects of ability grouping policies on educational achievement is inconsistent. Case studies of single schools have shown beneficial effects for pupils of average and below average ability (e.g. Gregson and Quin, 1978; Thompson, 1974). On the other hand an account by HMI was sceptical about the work of many mixed ability classes, claiming that it frequently failed to cater adequately for able pupils, and resulted in a restricted syllabus because teachers avoided activities they considered too difficult for less able pupils (DES, 1978b). The inspectors' criticism may have been justified. Unfortunately the somewhat impressionistic nature of their survey, combined with lack of detail both on their research methods and on the results, cannot inspire confidence in their conclusions.

Overall, the limited evidence suggest that:

(1) Mixed ability teaching has social benefits.
(2) It may enhance the educational progress of pupils of average ability and below.
(3) Its effect on pupils of above average ability remains very much an open question.

In a study at Banbury school in Oxfordshire, Newbold (1977) concluded that formal organisation, whether ability based or mixed ability, was less important than the role of the individual teacher. Another way of putting this is that differences between teachers are more important than differences in organisational policy.

In other words, the teacher's attitudes and behaviour towards pupils with learning difficulties are probably the critical factors, rather than the school's policy on ability grouping. Mastery learning, Dweck (1977) claims, helps pupils to regard failure as a useful learning experience rather than as an indication of personal inadequacy. In theory there is no reason why this should not be as possible in the 'D' stream as in the 'A' stream. Equally, there is no theoretical reason why teachers of 'D' stream classes should not value their pupils' achievements as highly as those of 'A' stream classes, nor why the 'D' stream's achievements should not be valued as highly by the school's senior management.

Nevertheless, the school's policy on ability grouping is likely to carry its own hidden agenda which in turn is likely to affect the attitudes and ultimately the behaviour of teachers. Selection by ability cannot easily avoid creating a hierarchy within the school, in which highest status is ascribed to pupils *and* their teachers at the top of the hierarchy and lowest status to those at the foot. It places at the heart of the school a competitive philosophy without recognising the essential contraction in this philosophy.

The contradiction is simply that each band, or stream receives a different curriculum, so that the initial selection process is rapidly 'justified' by the pupils' attainments. This occurs even when the upper and lower bands receive in theory a similar curriculum. In practice more is expected from the upper band. For example, more home-work is expected and failure to complete home-work is usually followed up more rigorously. By the end of the year the differences between the bands in attainment are almost inevitably wider than at the beginning.

Thus, selection by ability reflects an essentially competitive philosophy yet at the same time is self-maintaining. Teachers in low ability or special needs classes may emphasise the intrinsic nature of the task through an emphasis on mastery learning. They may even achieve a high level of success. Their success, however, will be in spite of, and not because of, the school's policy on academic organisation. The reason is that the teacher's emphasis on the intrinsic value of the work the pupils are doing is inconsistent with the dominant philosophy in the school which is likely to equate ability with status. Thus ability grouping exerts an active influence in the hidden curriculum. Mixed ability grouping will not necessarily result in any change in the hidden curriculum. Grouping by ability is, after all, quite a common strategy in mixed ability classes.

It does, however, create possibilities for changes which other systems impede.

Other Aspects of School Organisation

We have already seen several ways in which the school's formal organisation may make some of its own aims and objectives unattainable. Punctuality for lessons is invariably a stated objective, yet is unattainable when there is no gap between lessons or when children must come from the other end of the building, or even from a separate site (Rabinowitz, 1981). Class tutors may be expected to play an active part in the pastoral care network, yet be given no real opportunity to do so (Galloway, 1983). Teachers may intend flexible movement between bands or sets in the light of progress or difficulties pupils encounter, yet provide such different curricula to each group that such movement is effectively restricted to rare cases.

For children with special needs such inconsistencies may become even more damaging. A teacher's intention may be to meet needs identified through a formal assessment process, aiming to remediate the pupils' difficulties so that they will be able to return to ordinary classes. Such remedial activities may take place in a class for children with learning problems, or in a group for pupils presenting behaviour problems. The remedial programmes may be highly specialised and intrinsically admirable. Their aim, however, may for two reasons be defeated by the method, even though the method in itself may be beyond reproach. First, there is the problem of transfer; progress in one situation does not necessarily transfer, and hence cannot readily be used, in a different situation. Thus, progress achieved in a special group will not necessarily help a child on his return to ordinary classes. Second, however much progress children may make in the special group, they will still have missed a substantial amount of the curriculum covered while they were receiving special help. Their return, then, is associated with realistic anxiety about 'catching up', and consequent fear of further failure.

Discrimination against pupils with special needs can also occur in less obvious ways. Probably all schools intend that extra-curricula activities should be as accessible to pupils with special needs as to any other pupils. Indeed, teachers would probably assert that they might benefit from extra-curricula activities even more than their peers. Again, the reality of day-to-day activities can ensure that the intention is not fulfilled. In schools where the special needs department operates as a relatively self-contained unit, the teachers most actively involved with extra-curricula activities may seldom come into contact with pupils with special needs. In the absence of any co-ordinated effort to enlist their interest, they seldom take the initiative. Teachers may then assume that they are simply not interested, while in reality the organisation of curriculum and time-table have placed them at a disadvantage.

Looking at discipline in schools, it is generally easy to see strategies which are self-defeating, reinforcing the patterns of behaviour they are intended to discourage. When deviant behaviour is severe or frequent enough, the pupil could be regarded under the 1981 Education Act as having special needs. Punishment, though may enhance a pupil's status in the eyes of his peer group.

Reynolds *et al.* (1985) found no differences between nine Welsh secondary modern schools in the number of cigarettes pupils smoked out of school. Yet differences between schools in the amount of smoking that took place on school premises were substantial and were directly linked to the school's policy on smoking patrols: the more smoking patrols, the more smoking. As this did not generalise to smoking out of school, it is reasonable to conclude that the teachers' smoking patrols encouraged the very problem they were designed to reduce. Similarly, over-enthusiastic patrolling of lunch-time queues may encourage disruptive behaviour, especially if teachers themselves eat in a separate room from pupils.

To summarise, our argument has two strands. The first is that certain aspects of a school's policy may not be reflected in day-to-day practice. The second is that when policy is reflected in practice it may be implemented in a way which defeats its own purpose. In each case tensions are created for teachers as well as for pupils. These are inevitably reflected in the school's hidden curriculum.

Pupils with personal or educational problems, especially when they come from unsupportive homes, may be more deeply affected by a school's hidden curriculum than more able pupils or pupils with caring, articulate parents who take an active interest in their schooling. Hence, it is important to consider in more detail the network of relationships in school and how these can be modified or improved. The rest of this chapter considers three approaches to improving teacher:pupil interaction and teacher effectiveness. The next chapter looks more specifically at the needs of teachers themselves.

Behavioural Approaches

Overview

Behavioural approaches may, at first sight, seem an odd choice when discussing improvement in teacher-pupil interaction, though the emphasis on teacher effectiveness is obvious enough. On the other hand, a recurring theme in the literature is the improvement in a child's attitudes and relationships following improvement in behaviour or in academic skills.

Behavioural work in schools has its origin in animal learning experiments. Gradually experimental psychologists started to extend the principles they had demonstrated in the laboratory into work with children in schools and clinics. They also demonstrated that the terminology of learning theory could provide a useful framework to explain the interaction between teacher and pupils or between therapist and patient.

The rationale for behavioural work in schools is clear and relatively uncontroversial. Learning implies change; in developing new skills children are, by definition, acquiring new behaviours. In this sense, behavioural approaches can be seen as an attempt to help children to learn, or teachers to teach, more effectively. All teachers are concerned to provide conditions conducive to learning. At the simplest level, but one which is too frequently over-looked, this may involve attention to such things as the temperature in the classroom, the size of the desks or a flickering strip light. Yet it also involves dealing with behaviour problems which interfere with effective teaching and with learning strategies that restrict the child's progress. Again, all teachers are concerned with motivation. Another way of putting this is that effective teaching depends on successful identification and use of appropriate reinforcement.

Thus the aim of behavioural work in schools could be summarised as increasing teacher effectiveness. It involves planning and implementing programmes to deal with behavioural or learning difficulties, either of individuals or of the class as a whole. It may also involve programmes to develop or maintain a high level of motivation or concentration ('study behaviour' in the jargon of behaviourists).

Process

Typically, behavioural projects have six stages:

(1) Identifying behaviour which the teacher wishes to modify or which she wishes the child to acquire.
(2) Recording the frequency of the target behaviour, to provide a 'baseline' against which to measure subsequent progress.
(3) Analysis of events which precede the target behaviour (antecedents) and which follow it (consequences), the aim being to identify the events which act as a stimulus and as a reinforcement for the problem behaviour.
(4) Using this analysis to plan a programme to deal with the problem.
(5) Implementing the programme and maintaining records to monitor its effectiveness.
(6) Reviewing progress and if necessary revising or changing the programme.

In addition it is possible, at least in principle, to demonstrate the effectiveness of the programme by reverting to the baseline condition. For example, the initial analysis (stage 3 above) might have suggested that the pupils' inattentiveness to questions was associated with the teacher's impersonal commands or questions: 'Class IIIb, get out your books'. The programme might then have required the teacher to personalise instructions and questions, using a pupil's name. Having demonstrated an increase in attentiveness by comparison with the baseline, the teacher could revert to her original practice in order to check whether the improvement was in fact due to the programme. Research psychologists and journal editors like the teachers' control over behaviour to be demonstrated in this way. Not surprisingly, busy classroom teachers are less enthusiastic.

Most behavioural work in schools has its theoretical grounding in the principles of applied behavioural analysis. The six stages described above are based on these principles. The emphasis is quite explicitly on observed behaviour. This does not just imply that the target behaviour — i.e. the behaviour the teacher wishes to change — must be identified in precise, quantifiable terms. It also implies that the analysis of the problem is based on equally precise, quantifiable behaviours, i.e. the antecedents and consequences. In practice this means that the applied behavioural analysis focuses mainly, if not exclusively, on the setting in which the target behaviour occurs. This has led to a number of theoretical and practical problems which have severely limited the usefulness of much behavioural work.

Some Limitations

The emphasis on the control of observed behaviour has led to enthusiastic application of the techniques of behaviour modification. Unfortunately these have not always been based on a thorough analysis and understanding of the circumstances in which the techniques can be used appropriately. One eminent British psychologist has warned of the dangers of a 'mindless technology' (Berger, 1979). Another, while admitting that he had for ten years 'been attempting to proselytise among teachers, seeking to convert them, sometimes with a near evangelical zeal, to what I call "behavioural pedagogy" ', warned of the dangers of 'behavioural over kill' (Wheldall, 1982). By this he meant that teachers sometimes used unnecessarily 'heavy' techniques to deal with relatively minor problems, for example 'a full-scale token economy to stop one child picking his nose!'

Yet objections to much behavioural work go deeper than the misuse of behaviour modification techniques. Focusing on the context in which the problem occurs inevitably leads many teachers to overlook other factors which may be of equal, or greater relevance to the problem. The teacher's discipline techniques may be influenced by the prevailing attitudes in the staff-room. Family circumstances may have an important bearing on a child's classroom behaviour. Membership of a peer group whose members are in different classes may exert an important influence on what a pupil finds reinforcing in the classroom. Problem behaviour may also result from an inadequate or inappropriate curriculum rather than from direct aspects of teacher-pupil interaction.

Even when the analysis of the problem under observation is valid, the technical obstacles in behavioural work are formidable. Harrop (1980) has drawn attention to the difficulties in obtaining reliable baseline observations. It is implicit from his discussion that *no* practising educational psychologist and *no* practising teacher will have the time to obtain baseline observations of sufficient detail and reliability to satisfy the rigorous scientific requirements underpinning behavioural work. Apart from anything else, if baseline observations are not to be affected by individual idiosyncracies, at least two observers are needed and observations need to be carried out over a substantial period.

This does not mean that behavioural work has no place except as part of a carefully conducted and generously staffed research programme. It does mean that:

(1) The claims that observations are objective should be regarded with caution.
(2) Programmes may often be based on an insufficient analysis of the problem.
(3) Programmes may be implemented inappropriately, for example when a teacher fails, perhaps without realising the fact, to reinforce specified behaviour as required by a programme.
(4) The teacher may feel a sense of resentment and/or personal inadequacy when the programme is unsuccessful and reject behavioural approaches in future.

Another technical problem in applying behavioural approaches concerns the question of transfer. It is one thing for a teacher to change his reinforcement strategies in one context, for example to improve a pupil's concentration ('on-task' behaviour) in a maths lesson. It is quite another thing for the teacher to use the same principles when teaching a different class or a different subject. It is even less likely that the pupil's improved concentration will transfer to different subjects taught by different teachers. The problems have been clearly recognised (e.g. Kazdin, 1978) but behaviour analysts remain a long way from solving them. It may be that the experimental method on which they pride themselves is the greatest obstacle to the successful generalisation of skills acquired in behavioural programmes. The reason is that, in practice if not in theory, the experimental method in applied behavioural analysis encourages attention to a limited range of factors, whereas classroom behaviour is affected by an extremely wide range of variables.

In Sheffield we showed that some schools were outstandingly successful in preventing, rather than dealing with, disruptive behaviour (e.g. Galloway *et al.*, 1982a; Galloway, 1983). To the best of our knowledge behavioural approaches were used in none of the most successful schools. Nor is there evidence that systematic use of behavioural approaches characterised the most successful schools described by Rutter *et al.* (1979). This does not imply that applied behavioural analysis can make no contribution to school or class effectiveness. It does imply that many other factors are also relevant. This view is expressed succinctly by Berger (1982).

> Clinical, and increasingly, research experience (Rutter *et al.*, 1979) indicate that some proportion (if not a significant proportion) of classroom problems are influenced by a complex set of factors, interacting and changing over time. Only some of these stem from the class teacher's practices, practices which are the primary focus of behaviour analysis interventions. Yet, success in changing what class teachers do does not always lead to changes in the behaviour and cognitions of pupils, or in their academic capabilities and educational performance. Also, successful interventions have a circumscribed and transient impact — the problem of specificity of effects of behavioural interventions is well documented (Wahler, 1980; Kazdin, 1982). Finally, we have no systematic record of failures of behavioural interventions or such interventions with a narrower or other than intended outcome. These observations strongly suggest that behavioural analysis interventions only partially account for outcome variance. Other factors must be implicated in the genesis and maintenance of classroom problems and not just the behaviours of teachers or peers. (Berger, 1982, p. 292)

Implications

In the same article Berger argued that many of the limitations inherent in applied behavioural analysis could be overcome. Approaches derived from social learning theory, (e.g. Bandura, 1974; Bower and Hilgard, 1981), retain the theoretical assumption that much behaviour is learned, yet enable the psychologist or teacher to take account of factors which extend beyond immediate classroom observations. Such factors could include information on developmental problems of individual pupils, difficulties in social relationships, learning problems and so on.

Behavioural programmes, then, provide no panacea for dealing with the problems presented by pupils with special needs. Applied behavioural analysis in the classroom has served a valuable function in directing attention to important aspects of teachers' and pupil's behaviour, but Berger's conclusion that it 'has given us the lead but not the solution' indicates the need for caution. Planning a behavioural programme requires a thorough understanding of the importance of individual differences and of social relationships within the school and the classroom.

This does not mean that a behavioural analysis carried out in the classroom is unnecessary, but that it is only a starting point. Provision for children with special needs requires more than the piecemeal approach implicit in most behaviour modification projects, however valuable these may be in their own right. It requires an organisational framework and a climate which promote prosocial behaviour so that pupils' values are consistent with the stated aims of the school, facilitate attention to special needs in the curriculum and provide effective educational, personal and vocational guidance for all pupils. It is to the question of guidance that we must now turn.

Counselling: One Aspect of Guidance

Scope

Counselling implies that one person helps, or at least tries to help, another. Hence there is a sense in which all teachers require counselling skills at some level. A problem which all teachers have faced from time to time is pupils arriving late for school. Occasionally the child's explanation seems inadequate, and the teacher needs to enquire in more detail about the reasons for lateness. Possible explanations are that the pupil has overslept, that he had to finish homework, that he has to get a younger sibling up or take him to school, that he has to walk nearly three miles to school as his parents cannot afford the bus fare, that he has been bullied in the playground on days when he has arrived early, or that he particularly fears and dislikes the form tutor who takes the first session of the day. Establishing the reason is not always straightforward. It can require a high level of interviewing skill — particularly if the disliked form tutor is the interviewer!

There is not much point in the interview unless something is expected to happen as a result. Thus, the teacher can refer the child to someone else, for example a senior colleague, educational welfare officer or educational psychologist. More frequently, though, he will himself try to help the child deal with the problem. It could be argued that this constitutes advice-giving, which should be considered guidance rather than counselling. Certainly, it is not rare to find the term counselling reserved for one particular approach or group of approaches, for example, client-centred therapy (Rogers, 1951). It is difficult to justify this distinction. Counselling can utilise a range of methodologies, including behavioural analysis (e.g. Jehu *et al.*, 1972).

Nevertheless, there is a valid argument that counselling requires some conceptual framework, which distinguishes it from 'straight-forward' giving advice. Further, most teachers can identify children who, they think, might be helped by a specialist counsellor. There is less agreement on which children could be helped, what they might be helped to do or become, and how they might be helped to do it.

The wholly laudable recognition that some pupils have special needs which are not being met has encouraged policy makers in some countries to conclude that full-time counsellors should be appointed to all secondary schools. Part of the rationale is perhaps that some individual needs require a one-to-one relationship. Also, it is felt that some pupils' needs require a therapeutic relationship, either through individual or group counselling, which should be distinct from the school's disciplinary framework.

In fairness, it is important to add that these activities form at most only part of the work of school counsellors in countries such as the United States, Canada and New Zealand which have appointed them to all secondary schools. In addition they are involved with the school's educational and vocational guidance programmes. It remains true, though, that personal counselling is an important part of their work.

Bolger (1983) points out that counselling in schools and colleges in Britain spans barely two decades. The first training course started in 1965, and was rapidly followed by others. The most rapid growth in counselling was from 1969 – 1978, with a steady decline since them. Noting a continuing reduction in the number of counsellors in secondary schools in Britain, Murgatroyd (1983) pointed out that counselling courses too were 'collapsing like a supernova into the black hole of London, given that (courses at) Swansea, Exeter, Huddersfield, Keele and Aston have either closed or are closing'.

It seems plausible that course closures partially reflect declining demand from secondary schools for counsellors. They also reflect the economic pressures on universities which resulted in many staff being encouraged to take early retirement. It is certainly true, though, that counselling never gained the general acceptance in British schools that it gained in other countries.

To some extent this reflected the organisation of education in Britain. In New Zealand, for example the Minister of Education could announce a national policy to create a counsellor post at each secondary school. Governors and head teachers in Britain guard jealously their right to employ and deploy staff. Insisting on a particular type of appointment might have been seen as a serious threat to their autonomy. The fact remains, though, that head teachers were by no means universally in favour of appointing counsellors.

Increasing financial restrictions undoubtedly had something to do with this. A gradually changing climate in education, inimical to radical developments in the field of personal relationships, probably also contributed. Yet sound educational reasons can also be put forward against the appointment of specialist counsellors in schools. Seven arguments are often given. They are summarised here as we deal with issues that arise from them in more detail later.

(1) It is maintained that all teachers should be involved in a school's guidance network, and that to identify one as a specialist counsellor is inconsistent with this policy. Some counselling skills, as we have already argued, are required as part of routine teaching responsibilities, so the emphasis should be on staff development through the school rather than on creating an elite.

(2) Following from this point, a counsellor's work can seem inconsistent with the school's broader aims. This can happen in two ways. First, the counsellor's 'client-centred' approach and emphasis on personal growth may be interpreted as placing a relatively low priority on the child's general behaviour and progress in school. Second, and perhaps more serious, the existence of a full-time counsellor can reduce the commitment which form tutors and subject teachers might otherwise feel to deal with problems themselves: referring a problem to the counsellor is much easier than finding a way to deal with it oneself, at least in the short term.

(3) A single person has neither the knowledge nor the time to provide a range of personal, educational and vocational guidance that should be an integral part of the life and work of any school. Nor is it realistic to regard the counsellor as co-ordinator, or leader of a guidance team. Guidance should be so central to the school's activities that the lead must come from the head and the senior

management. In practice the counsellor's status within the school denies him the opportunity to fill this leadership role.

(4) The basis for guidance — personal, educational and vocational — lies in classroom teaching, as part of the guidance or pastoral curriculum. It is unrealistic, and undesirable, to think that guidance must always be offered on an individual basis. Here again, the involvement of all teachers in a guidance network is emphasised.

(5) Professional development, particularly in the helping and teaching professions requires day-to-day contact with colleagues. Although trained originally as teachers, school counsellors often see themselves, and are seen by their colleagues, primarily as counsellors rather than as teachers. Hence they can quickly become professionally isolated in the staff-room, leading to reliance for professional support on similarly isolated colleagues in other schools.

(6) This can lead to some disturbing ambiguities and conflicts. In New Zealand, for example, counsellors are frequently involved in testing pupils on entry to secondary school for allocation to ability based streams (*see* p. 56). On the basis of the test results, Maori pupils are often placed in low streams. Recognising that they have been ascribed low status within the school, dismissed as public examination prospects in schools which regard public examinations as their principal goal, many Maori pupils develop the familiar problems associated with disaffection from school. When they become big enough problems to the system they are likely to be referred for counselling.

Counsellors see their job as promoting healthy development. Most of them have deep personal convictions against racism and against policies which discriminate against socially disadvantaged groups in society. They would indignantly refute a suggestion that they help to promote, rather than to meet, special educational needs. Yet many are active and frequently willing participants in a process which does just that. By refusing to take part they would find themselves in conflict with a central aspect of the school's policy. Worse, they would find themselves socially isolated in the staff-room. They would not need to be told that a counsellor who is isolated in the staff-room has little hope of influencing his colleagues' attitudes on behaviour. There is little doubt that counsellors in British schools found themselves in a similar 'double bind' — a situation in which they could not win.

(7) Observation in New Zealand schools, consistent reports from teachers in Nigerian schools which have appointed a counsellor, and comments from teachers in British schools are entirely consistent on one point. The group of pupils referred in largest numbers to the school counsellor is of disruptive pupils. It is equally clear that the counsellor is expected to do something to change these pupils' behaviour. Unfortunately disruptive pupils constitute the one group whose behaviour is unlikely to change as a result of personal counselling. This has been clear since Levitt (1963) reviewed 22 studies on the results of psychotherapy. He showed that children presenting socially disruptive problems such as delinquency were much less likely to improve during or after psychotherapy than children with readily identified symptoms such as school phobia.

Levitt's conclusions have been challenged (e.g. Hood-Williams, 1960. Wright *et al.*, 1976). Other studies, however, both in America (Robins, 1966, 1972) and in Britain (Mitchell and Rosa, 1981) have shown that children seen for anti-social behaviour have a poor long-term prognosis particularly when compared with children receiving child guidance clinic treatment for 'neurotic' disturbance. Overall, the conclusion is clear: the pupils that teachers most frequently refer to counsellors are precisely the pupils whose behaviour is least likely to change as a result of counselling.

Conclusions

We do not wish to deny here that counter-arguments may be found to each of the seven objections just described. Individual counsellors have made a valuable contribution in many schools. Some have defined their job, or had it defined for them, largely in terms of personal or group counselling with pupils with problems. Others have seen their major responsibilities lying in different fields, such as assessment and testing, or vocational guidance. Occasionally, but less frequently than counsellors might wish, they have been seen as leaders, or co-ordinators of the school's guidance network. More often they have played an important part within the guidance network (e.g. A. Jones, 1980).

Our aim has been not so much to present arguments against appointing school counsellors, than to identify factors which initially inhibited growth in the school counselling movement and subsequently led to its decline. Perhaps the most important were realising that:

(1) A counsellor would not be able, on his own, to solve the problems presented by problem pupils.
(2) A counsellor was no substitute for an effective guidance network.
(3) Neither their training nor their status within the school equipped them to co-ordinate such a network.
(4) Therefore, counsellors could, at best, contribute to the guidance network, which might operate quite effectively without them.

The first three of these factors imply unrealistic expectations of what counsellors could offer. It may be that counsellors were the victim of other people's unrealistic expectations, or just that they failed to communicate what they could offer. In either case, fundamental questions remained about the nature, scope and quality of the school's guidance, or pastoral network.

Pastoral Case

Aims and Definitions

The term pastoral care is used to refer to the guidance network in schools in Britain. The broad aim of pastoral care is to promote the personal, educational and vocational development of all pupils in the school. These three areas are, of course, interrelated. Hamblin (1978) has defined pastoral care as:

> . . . that element in the teaching process which centres around the personality of the pupil and the forces in his environment which either facilitate or impede the development of intellectual and social skills, and foster or retard emotional stability . . . (it) is also concerned with the modification of the learning environment, adapting it to meet the needs of individual pupils, so that every pupil has the maximum chance of success whatever his background or general ability (p. xv).

It is clear from this definition that pastoral care is seen as an integral aspect of everything which happens in the school. As such, the pastoral network affects, and is affected by the school's general climate. Nor, for two reasons, can pastoral care sensibly be seen as separate and distinct from what happens in the formal academic curriculum.

First, Hamblin's definition specifically draws attention to the possible need for 'modification of the learning environment'. Teachers in senior or middle management positions with responsibility for pastoral care must, therefore, be concerned with tensions arising from the school's curriculum organisation. We have already identified many of these, for example, the isolation of full-time remedial classes and of behavioural units, difficulties on return to ordinary lessons after withdrawal for help in specific areas, and lack of support for teachers of mixed ability classes. Together, these three examples illustrate the importance of school policy and organisation, curriculum content, and in-service training and support for teachers. For senior teachers responsible for pastoral care to spend their time dealing with the curriculum's casualties is, at best, silly.

Second, pastoral care cannot be divorced from effective teaching. The pastoral element in effective teaching is no longer really controversial. The opening sentences of Dickens' novel 'Hard Times' caricatures one concept of teaching: 'Now what I want is Facts. Teach these boys and girls nothing but Facts. Facts alone are wanted in life. Plant nothing else and root out everything else.' Schools have come a long way since them. An interactive model of teaching, which conceptualises teaching as a process of interaction between teacher and pupils, is not seriously disputed. By definition, effective teaching implies successful learning, though not necessarily only of facts. Effective teaching implies among other things, that the teacher is:

(1) Able to present material in a way which interests and stimulates the pupils.
(2) Sensitive to differences between pupils in ability, temperament and interests.
(3) Able to use this sensitive awareness to motivate them, bearing in mind that different pupils respond to different kinds of motivation.

It is clear, then, that effective teaching requires an understanding of individual differences. In a large secondary school, in which a pupil may be taught by up to 12 teachers each week, it is equally clear that there has to be some procedure for co-ordinating and disseminating information about pupils. This constitutes an important facet in each school's pastoral care system, but by no means the only one.

Our discussion of the pastoral aspects of effective teaching also draws attention to a central aspect of pastoral care, namely its developmental nature. Pupils' general development is at least as much the responsibility of teachers responsible for pastoral care as of any other teachers. This is especially true of pupils with special needs, whose social and education development is, by definition, a matter for particular concern. It is slightly odd that this needs saying. The reason is that the gap between the 'conventional wisdom' about pastoral care and the reality is disturbingly wide.

In the most detailed and readily accessible account of pastoral care in an English secondary school, Best *et al.* (1983) describe a meeting of House heads in which teachers considered such topics as completion of forms from the County Careers Service, representatives on the Parent Teacher Association, fire drill, the 'signing-out book' for pupils leaving the school before the end of the day, and so on. The authors discussed this meeting in the light of conventional wisdom about pastoral care, as reflected both in standard books on the subject (e.g. Marland, 1974; Haigh, 1975) and in the formally stated aims and procedures of the school itself. Yet in the meeting of teachers with specific responsibility for pastoral care there was clearly:

> . . . a *prima facie* case for suspecting that some, at least, of the 'conventional wisdom' is neither an entirely true description of what 'pastoral care' is, nor a wholly realistic prescription for what it ought to be. (Best *et al.*, 1983, p. 29).

Many of the activities regarded as 'pastoral' in secondary schools have always taken place in the best schools. We have argued that pastoral care is an essential aspect in effective teaching, and are certainly not arguing that this is the prerogative of schools with an organised pastoral care system. Yet it was only with the reorganisation of secondary education into a comprehensive system that pastoral care was put on to a formal footing.

A Hidden Agenda

The stated aims of pastoral care imply benefits for pupils. Yet as always when new procedures are established, there was also a hidden agenda. Some of the items on the hidden agenda for creating pastoral care networks were:

(1) Giving the head of the secondary modern school subject departments the 'consolation prize' of head of year when the grammar school head of department became h.o.d. in the new comprehensive.
(2) Providing an alternative career ladder to the traditional one through subject departments.
(3) Creating a system concerned with 'problems of social control and administrative convenience' (Best *et al.*, 1977).
(4) Responding to teachers' short-term needs by providing middle management specialists to whom problem children could be referred; in addition, the newly created specialists could also act as a filter for referrals to agencies outside the school, and could take substantial responsibility for decisions on ability grouping, or referral to what was then called the remedial department.

While grammar schools now no longer provide departmental heads for comprehensives, the other items on the hidden agenda for pastoral care remain as relevant today as in the early days of comprehensive reorganisation. Marland (1983) refers to five fallacies of pastoral care:

(1) It requires no intellectual or theoretical background or knowledge.
(2) It is concerned primarily with responding to problems.
(3) It is not only primarily but totally concerned with individual casework.
(4) It has no content and is separate from the curriculum.
(5) It is to do with working only with pupils.

These five fallacies clearly imply a 'negative net' model of pastoral care. Implicitly, pastoral specialists have low status, at least compared with subject specialists. They are concerned mainly with pupils with special needs, but their involvement is essentially on a one-to-one basis, tagged on in some vague kind of way to the main body of the school's work.

No-one would deny that pastoral care should pay particular attention to pupils with special needs. Nor would anyone deny that all pupils require personal, educational and vocational guidance in order to make realistic choices and to benefit from what the school has to offer. In theory pastoral care has always been concerned with all pupils. In practice, pastoral specialists have too frequently allowed their time and energy to be monopolised by pupils with special needs. The irony is that this is in the interests neither of pupils with special needs nor of the majority.

The uncontroversial need for a whole school approach to pastoral care again indicates the limitations in Marland's five fallacies. Marland (1983) himself sees the nature and delivery of pastoral care in radically different terms. He argues that:

(1) It requires a substantial knowledge base.
(2) It requires careful planning.
(3) Group and tutorial work have a central role.
(4) Attention should be paid to the *content* of pastoral care.
(5) Heads of house or year must work through their teams of tutors, rather than attempt to do individual casework themselves.

Pastoral Methods and Pastoral Curriculum

Perhaps the greatest single problem in pastoral care is that attention has focused mainly on the organisation of pastoral care rather than on the pastoral content of what the school teaches. In practice, teachers frequently see pastoral care as a hierarchical network, headed by the deputy head (pastoral) and filtering down to the form tutor. We have already seen how the organisation of a pastoral care network may defeat the network's own aims, when discussing the role of secondary school form tutors and primary school class teachers (chapter 5). A related issue is how the roles and responsibilities of individuals in the network can lead heads and deputies to overlook important issues in the content of pastoral work.

The basic organisation of the pastoral network, then, is far from straightforward. Yet providing a coherent organisational structure is not on its own sufficient. Indeed the more elaborate the pastoral network, the greater the danger of overlooking the pastoral content in the school's curriculum. Pupils need a range of information and skills in order to make realistic decisions and to make the best use of the school's resources. In an important article, Marland (1980) refers to this as the pastoral curriculum. He argues that teachers should identify the information and skills which need to be taught under the broad headings of personal, educational and vocational guidance. These will include such diverse elements as rights and obligations as an adolescent or young adult, study skills and use of the library, and making constructive use of feedback from teachers.

Having agreed, at least in principle, on the content of the pastoral curriculum it becomes possible to consider how it may be implemented. This will involve a programme of tutorial work, but should also involve existing subject departments and the use of specialist teachers. Library and study skills, for example, may well be taught at some stage by specialists, though some preliminary teaching could have taken place in the tutorial programme. Subject teachers, however, will probably need to reinforce or adapt the specialists' work in order to ensure that skills acquired in one context transfer to another.

Good Practice: Evidence and Theory

Research on the effectiveness of pastoral care is conspicuous by its absence. There is an urgent need for analysis of ways in which pastoral care may contribute to, or impede the school's success in achieving its aims. We have already suggested when discussing the form tutor's role that the organisation of pastoral care may be self-defeating. The same study attempted to identify characteristics of pastoral care at four schools with remarkably low rates of disruptive behaviour (Galloway, 1983). Seven characteristics were identified:

(1) The underlying philosophy, from the head down was that the aim of pastoral care was to enhance the child's progress and adjustment at school rather than to deal with problems out of school.
(2) Each school regarded the distinction between discipline and pastoral care as spurious.
(3) Referring problem pupils to senior staff was discouraged.
(4) On the other hand, senior staff *were* readily available for advice and assistance in helping teachers deal with problems themselves.
(5) The class tutor's importance was recognised.
(6) Regular and generally informal contact was established with parents.
(7) Teachers tended to regard behaviour and learning difficulties as *teaching* problems; as such, they expected to be able to solve them, if necessary with help from colleagues or

from outside agencies; at other schools these pupils were regarded as learning problems or behaviour problems with the implication that, as the problem lay 'in' the child, teachers could be expected to do little about it.

This kind of analysis is undoubtedly very limited. The research focused exclusively on schools with low or high rates of disruptive behaviour. We made no attempt to analyse curriculum content in the schools concerned. It was clear, though, from this study and from the rest of the research programme (Galloway *et al.*, 1982*a*), that the nature and quality of pastoral care reflected, for better or worse, the school's overall climate. Thus, the pastoral process could individualise problems, regarding pupils' special needs as evidence of personal or familial inadequacy. Yet it could also contribute powerfully to a climate in which special needs were seen as evidence of a need to review teaching method or curriculum content.

A wide-ranging pastoral curriculum supported by a coherent pastoral network caters for all pupils. It remains true, though that pupils with special needs will require particular attention from the pastoral team. This is partly because of the curriculum implications of their needs, and partly because their parents are less likely than those of other pupils to seek frequent contact with teachers about their educational progress. The paradox is that effective pastoral care for pupils with special needs is only possible within a climate which provides it for the majority as well.

Conclusions

We have argued in this chapter that school policy and school climate can contribute to, if not cause, problems which the Warnock Committee regarded as evidence of special educational need. We have also argued that school policy and climate may:

(1) Inhibit expression of these problems.
(2) Help teachers to recognise and meet special needs.

The school's formal organisation contributes to school climate, but only indirectly. It provides a framework which facilitates or inhibits development but cannot itself produce change in attitudes or practice.

The various approaches we have discussed, behavioural methods, counselling and pastoral care, may each help to influence a school's climate. Unfortunately they can also mask deficiencies both in climate and in organisation. In other words, they can be employed to maintain an unsatisfactory *status quo*.

Teachers with pastoral responsibilities nevertheless have considerable opportunity to influence school climate, particularly in their capacity as leaders of a pastoral team. Moreover, an effective guidance, or pastoral care, network will ensure that a pupil's special needs are recognised and met. The way that teachers approach their pastoral responsibilities can create a climate which accepts exceptionality, ensures that the achievements of pupils with special needs are valued, and creates opportunities for them to contribute, and be seen to be contributing, to the school community. The way teachers approach pastoral care can also create a climate in which exceptionality is resented. Whether it is accepted or resented may depend on how well the school caters for its teachers, providing *them* with pastoral care and opportunities for personal and professional development.

7 THE SPECIAL EDUCATIONAL NEEDS OF TEACHERS

Introduction

If, as a recent report on London schools (ILEA, 1984) implied, schools often cater inadequately for most pupils of below average intelligence, it becomes unrealistic to expect them to be any more successful with pupils who have special needs. Another way of looking at what schools offer their pupils is to ask what they offer their teachers. Neither the Warnock Report nor the 1981 Education Act emphasised the personal needs of teachers. Yet teachers who feel bored, lack job satisfaction or are experiencing the negative effects of stress cannot sensibly be expected to produce interested, alert pupils who take pride in their school and in their own achievements.

The Warnock Report called for a special education element in initial teacher training. The committee also advocated salary recognition for 'a range of recognised qualifications in special education, to be obtained at the end of a one-year full-time course or its equivalent' as well as a range of in-service courses. Admirable though these recommendations are, they do not in themselves tackle the question of stress and job-satisfaction in teaching. No analysis of children's special needs can afford to overlook such issues, for the straightforward reason that children with special needs frequently become the focus for stress and for lack of job satisfaction. They are seen as the cause of problems which may not in fact be of their own making. Once seen in this light their behaviour and progress are likely to deteriorate. The conclusion, in itself legitimate, may then be that they have special needs. Yet the problems they present may be the product of their teacher's needs.

This chapter reviews the notions of stress and of satisfaction in teaching, with particular reference to the presence of children with special needs. We discuss evidence that the nature and amount of stress, and of job-satisfaction, have little to do with any objectively describable pupil characteristics. Rather, they depend on other factors which are to a considerable extent independent of the pupil intake. We discuss the nature of some of these factors, with particular reference to teacher support networks within the school and to staff development.

Stress and Satisfaction in Teaching

In our research in Sheffield we asked a random sample of teachers from each of ten secondary schools to 'describe the last incident in which a pupil or group of pupils presented you with any real problem' (Galloway *et al.*, 1982*a*). The ten schools varied widely both in their exclusion rates and in the general behaviour of pupils as observed during the research. The teachers' responses varied just as widely, but the variation was as wide between schools as between individual teachers within a school.

The differences between schools were reflected both in the recency and in the seriousness of the incidents described. Thus at one school half the teachers we interviewed could think of no incident causing them real concern in the current school year. In two other schools, 85 per cent of teachers reported incidents that had caused them real concern in the current year. Some teachers in all schools reported relatively minor incidents, for example:

A fourth year boy; he just tended to wander around the lab, doing little work if any. It wasn't a discipline situation, but he would make adverse comments.

In such cases the teacher seemed to have felt in control of the situation. It was not associated with severe feelings of stress. Incidents of this sort were the norm in some schools: most teachers could recall them but they did not seriously interfere with day-to-day teaching. In a minority of schools the picture was different, with several teachers recalling incidents which 'were either more serious, or were symptomatic of a prolonged struggle, indicating an advanced state of exhausted frustration, often with an accompanying sense of futility':

It was this morning — not a major problem — it's an on-going one. They all are — something you deal with week in, week out. He had a rubber band he'd been flicking the other kids with. And he'd been smoking on the way to school this morning. He'd been on report twice before. The first time he lost the report form, and the second one he hasn't brought back to me yet — he was ill last week, so I gave him a third. (pp. 139 – 40)

The impression, strikingly, was that the schools were providing radically different experiences not only for their pupils, but also for their teachers. Further, the differences could not be attributed to factors in the catchment areas. We had always taken for granted that children's behaviour and lack of progress could create stress for teachers. Our interviews with teachers, however, convinced us that disruptive behaviour, with its associated lack of progress for many of the pupils concerned, could frequently result from teacher stress. The stress, moreover, arose from the social and professional climate of the school, and not from factors outside the school, however important they might be in their own right.

Some Problems of Definition

Stress

An immediate problem in saying that stress can arise from, or be inhibited by, the school's social and professional climate is that this assumes a particular definition of stress. There are three major approaches to the study of stress. An 'engineering' model sees stress as pressures imposed on teachers by aspects of their work, and investigates the nature of these pressures. In contrast a 'physiological' model focuses on the teacher's responses to events or situations at work. This model assumes a correlation between stress and health. Thus, two immediate responses to stress are sweating and release of adrenalin into the blood stream. Medium term responses may be increased susceptibility to colds, migraines or minor infections, often reflected in increased teacher absences towards the end of term. Long term responses may be increased susceptibility to coronary heart disease, peptic ulcer or diabetes.

The limitation in the engineering model is that it cannot account for individual differences between teachers. Behaviour which one teacher finds extremely stressful may be seen in a quite different light by another. Similarly, the physiological model is limited by its concentration on individual responses to stress. Cox (1978) favoured an interactive model, seeing stress 'as part of a complex and dynamic system of transactions between the person and his environment'. This acknowleges the importance both of individual responses and of external pressures. It was developed by Kyriacou and Sutcliffe (1978) who proposed that:

> Teacher stress may be defined as a response of negative effect
> . . . resulting from aspects of the teacher's job and mediated by
> the perception that the demands made upon the teacher con-
> stitute a threat to his self esteem or well-being, and by coping
> mechanisms activated to reduce the perceived threat. (p. 6)

In this definition, stress arises when the teacher perceives
demands as a threat to self-esteem or well-being. In addition, stress
is experienced when 'coping mechanisms' are unable to deal with
the perceived threat. Translating this into the classroom, a pupil
who consistently shouts answers to the teacher's question when
another pupil has been asked to speak is a potential source of
stress. How stressful the pupil actually is may depend on the extent
to which:

(1) The teacher sees the behaviour as a threat to his status in the
classroom.
(2) He can deal with the problem himself, with or without
guidance or assistance from colleagues.

Ways of coping with stress should not, then, be seen only in
terms of the individual teacher's own personal or professional
resources. To see them in this light would be as one-sided as seeing
children's special needs solely in terms of results from individual
testing. A child's needs present themselves in the school and
classroom context and, to some extent, are the product of that context. Similarly, the way a teacher deals with potentially stressful
situations will not just depend on the teacher's personality and
training. It will also depend on the personal and material resources
available within the school, and on the unwritten expectation of
colleagues.

Satisfaction

The concept of satisfaction is at least as complex as that of stress.
There is a high negative correlation between job satisfaction and
stress reported by teachers (Kyriacou and Sutcliffe, 1979) but this
does not mean that every teacher who reports a lot of stress will
also report low job satisfaction. Nor can we assume that high job
satisfaction will necessarily enhance performance in the classroom.

The relationship is highly controversial: a sense of job satisfaction may enhance performance; on the other hand, feeling that you are doing a good job may be an important source of satisfaction (Galloway *et al.*, 1985). It seems more likely that there is an interactive relationship. While job satisfaction will not necessarily help a person become a better teacher, consistent lack of satisfaction at work may be associated with frustration, and ultimately with the apathy associated with 'burn-out' (Edelwich and Brodsky, 1980).

This raises the question whether satisfaction should be seen as a need, or as an end state. Is satisfaction, in other words, a concept which teachers are motivated to achieve, or a description of a current feeling? From a research point of view, at least for present purposes, the latter is more useful. We are interested in the sources of satisfaction, and in the factors which promote or reduce satisfaction from teaching.

Investigating the sources of satisfaction requires a distinction between overall satisfaction and 'facet' satisfaction (Lawler, 1974 and Holdaway, 1978). Lawler regarded facet satisfaction as 'people's affective reactions to particular aspects of the job'. If we are interested in which teachers experience high, or low, job satisfaction, there is evidence that we must consider a wide range of possible sources of satisfaction, rather than overall satisfaction (Galloway *et al.*, 1985).

To complicate matters still further, the sources of satisfaction and of dissatisfaction may be separate and distinct. When completing questionnaires, teachers who report low overall satisfaction often rate as their main sources of satisfaction the same items as teachers who report high overall satisfaction at work. Herzberg *et al.* (1959) argued that job satisfaction was associated with aspects of the job which met the individual's need for personal, or psychological growth. He emphasised the importance of the intrinsic aspects of the job. In a teacher's case examples might be seeing children make progress, establishing good relationships with children, and working with a team of colleagues. The main sources of dissatisfaction, in contrast, arose from conditions at work rather than from the work itself. Thus, low salary and lack of ancillary support might be seen as contributing to dissatisfaction at work.

The 'two factor' theory has been criticised (e.g. Schmidt, 1976; Wolf, 1970). On the other hand Sergiovanni (1967) has confirmed its general usefulness in analysing interviews with teachers, and Holdaway (1978) when analysing questionnaire responses. For present purposes the implication is that the sources of job satisfaction may be similar, irrespective of the teacher's overall level of satisfaction. So may the sources of dissatisfaction. Thus, when we consider highly rated sources of satisfaction we are considering things of importance to all teachers, or at least to most, and not just to teachers who report high satisfaction at work.

Sources of Stress and of Satisfaction

The factors emerging as the main sources of stress or of satisfaction depend on the questions researchers ask teachers. They also depend both on how the results are analysed and on how they are interpreted. Simpson (1962, 1976), for example, showed that absence rates were highest amongst teachers in their first years in the profession. The attendance of men, but not women, improved markedly in the 25 – 39 year old age-range. Young teachers, still learning the job, may well experience more stress than experienced colleagues. Similarly, teachers aged 25 – 39 are in the promotion bracket, and may not wish to reduce their chances by frequent absences. On the other hand, the relationship between teachers' absence rates and the amount of stress they report is weak (e.g. Galloway *et al.*, 1984*b*). Moreover, showing that a particular group of teachers is 'at risk' is not the same as showing the circumstances in which each group experiences stress.

Another problem in considering sources of stress is to distinguish the effect of national or l.e.a. policy decisions from the effects of policy decisions at school level. Dunham (1976, 1977) regarded the social and emotional upheaval of secondary school reorganisation into a comprehensive system as a major source of stress. Associated with this reorganisation, teachers found themselves in two kinds of role conflict. Pressure from colleagues, for example, to retain ability banding or to adopt mixed ability classses, could lead to 'intra-role conflict'. 'Inter-role conflict', on the other hand, could occur when teachers could not reconcile conflicting roles. Staff with pastoral responsibilities and teachers responsible for children with special needs are particularly susceptible to this sort of pressure.

Several studies have drawn attention to the importance of relationships with colleagues. Holdaway (1978) found a generally high level of satisfaction with relationships with colleagues amongst teachers in Canada. Rudd and Wiseman (1962), in contrast, reported British teachers as identifying poor relationships with colleagues amongst the most important sources of dissatisfaction. Similarly, Coates and Thoresen (1976) reviewed several studies showing tensions in relationships with senior colleagues as major sources of anxiety for beginning teachers. These research results are not necessarily inconsistent. Teachers may derive satisfaction from relationships with most of their colleagues, yet experience stress or anxiety over their contact with particular individuals.

In a study of 196 primary teachers in New Zealand we distinguished between stress associated with curriculum areas, stress associated with events that occurred infrequently, such as class trips, and stress associated with typical day-to-day events (Galloway *et al.*, 1982*b*, 1982*c*). The core curriculum areas of reading and maths were associated with quite a lot of stress or extreme stress by more than 17 per cent of teachers. However, 28 per cent reported quite a lot of stress or extreme stress from parent-teacher interviews for discussion of a child's progress, and 30 per cent from class trips. It would seem, therefore, that the curriculum is less frequently an important source of stress than situations potentially involving inter-personal conflict or situations potentially involving problems of pupil management and control.

This impression was strengthened by analysis of day-to-day events associated with stress. Pratt (1978) found children's behaviour and progress the most highly rated sources of stress from day-to-day events in a sample of Sheffield primary teachers. We adapted Pratt's stress-inventory in our New Zealand study. The ten most highly rated items, from a total of 46 are shown in *Table 7.1*. For comparison purposes we also show the ten most highly rated sources of satisfaction. These were provided by the same teachers, from responses to a modified version of Holdaway's (1978) *Satisfaction with Teaching Questionnaire*.

The Stress Inventory responses confirm that children's behaviour (items ranked 1, 2, 5, 6, 7 and 10) and educational progress items, 3, 4 and 9 are the most important sources of stress from day-to-day classroom events. This is consistent with Pratt's (1978) original conclusion that teacher-child interaction is 'the central and most enduring source of stress to most teachers'. It also suggests that children with special needs, whose behaviour and/or progress, are almost by definition, particularly disturbing to teachers, are a frequent cause of stress in day-to-day classroom teaching.

Table 7.1: Most Highly Rated Items on Stress Inventory for Teachers and on Satisfaction with Teaching Questionnaire

Stress Inventory for Teachers	Satisfaction with Teaching Questionnaire
Rank Items most highly rated as sources of stress	Rank Items most frequently identified as sources of satisfaction
(1) There was at least one problem child in my class	(1) Your relationship with pupils
(2) Some children did not do as they were told straight away	(2) Your relationship with other teachers
(3) I was not able to do enough with individual pupils	(3) Your freedom to select teaching methods
(4) The children did not listen to what was said	(4) The time-tabling of the programme/activities
(5) A child did not do as I told him/her to	(5) Your freedom to select subject matter for your class(es)
(6) Children made a lot of noise during this lesson/activity	(6) The number of hours you teach every week
(7) Some children were hostile and aggressive to each other	(7) Your relationship with senior staff in the school
(8) I was interrupted by other people/events	(=8) The level of pupil achievement in your class(es)
(9) Children had difficulties in learning/understanding	(=8) Your allocation to teaching a particular class/unit
(10) The weather made the children restless	(10) The general behaviour of pupils in your class(es)

Turning to the right hand side of *Table 7.1*, we see that children's behaviour (item 10) and children's progress (= 8) are also amongst the most highly rated sources of satisfaction. Further, the item ranked first ('your relationship with pupils') implies acceptable behaviour, while five other items could be seen as facilitating pupils' progress (items 3, 4, 5, 6 and = 8). At first sight it seems surprising that the most highly rated sources of stress and the most highly rated sources of satisfaction should be so similar. Looking at what actually happens in schools and staffrooms, though, the similarity is less surprising.

A teacher may feel considerable satisfaction over the behaviour and progress of most pupils, but feel a lot of stress in connection with a minority. Similarly, relationships with colleagues may provide an essential source of satisfaction at work, yet contact with one or two senior colleagues may prove a continuing source of friction. Teachers in an American survey overwhelmingly regarded school principals as the people who could do most to help reduce stress-related illness (Landsman, 1978). By implication, they could also do a great deal to induce such illness.

Table 7.1 shows the importance of relationships with children and with colleagues in teachers' job satisfaction. It also suggests the centrality of pupils with special needs as sources of stress. At one level, though, teachers may derive some encouragement from the most highly ranked sources of stress. Children's disturbing behaviour features prominently in the list. Yet children's behaviour is strongly affected by factors within the school. As we have argued repeatedly, there is nothing inevitable about disruptive behaviour in schools. We now need to consider how teacher support networks within schools may exacerbate, or inhibit, potentially destructive experience of stress.

Support Networks Within Schools

Replying to an open-ended question, at the end of the *Satisfaction with Teaching Questionnaire*, about main sources of dissatisfaction, one teacher wrote:

> Negative leadership from above . . . not being consulted or informed when any parent makes an inquiry about their child in my syndicate*; finding that the principal has told a parent that the child should be achieving a certain level and that the reason for failing to do this lies in the lack of teaching. (Galloway *et al.*, 1982*b*, p. 139)

* Group of classes for which the teacher was responsible.

This quotation illustrates an important point about professional relationships and their effect on how teachers interpret what happens in the classroom. A parent 'enquiring' of the head about a child's progress is potentially a source of stress. If the head or deputy happens to pass the window at the precise moment that Johnny, the most difficult child in the class, is throwing a piece of paper across the room, this is also potentially a source of stress. The teacher's actual perception of each incident will depend largely on the anticipated reaction from the head. Will the parent's enquiry result in professional denigration, as in the above example, or in constructive discussion to establish whether the parent's concern is justified, and if so what can be done about it? Will the head make a sarcastic public comment at the mid-morning tea break, or will he see the paper-throwing incident as part of a continuing problem which it is his job to help the teacher solve?

One of the characteristics of the four schools with exceptionally low rates of disruptive behaviour in the Sheffield and New Zealand studies was a tendency to discourage referral to senior members of staff (Galloway, 1983). Teachers were generally expected to deal with problems themselves. At some other schools teachers expected, and were expected, to refer problems to a senior colleague. In the short term this was helpful: responsibility could be passed to someone else. In the long term it was profoundly unhelpful. The senior colleague might punish the pupil, counsel him, or make enquiries about the home background. None of these courses of action would do anything to help the teacher deal with similar problems in future. The implication behind referral was no less clear for being unstated: the referring teacher lacked either the experience or competence to deal with the problem himself.

In some schools the situation was aggravated by a spurious distinction between discipline problems and emotional, or pastoral, problems. Subject teachers were expected to refer discipline problems to the head of department and pastoral problems to the head of year. The person required to decide between discipline and pastoral problems could be a subject teacher seeing the pupil only once a week. Not surprisingly, treatment in these circumstances was haphazard, depending not on the pupils' needs but on the unco-ordinated and idiosyncratic perceptions of his teachers. Again not surprisingly, it led to frustration and resentment for pupils and teachers alike.

The tendency in some schools with low rates of disruptive behaviour to discourage referral to senior staff did not imply that teachers lacked support. On the contrary, senior staff saw their job as helping colleagues to deal effectively with children's learning or behavioural problems. One head teacher commented that the real indication of failure was not needing help, but rather failing to ask for it. At this school the special needs department was explicitly organised to provide material and personal support for subject teachers. Each department had its own resource bank of materials, prepared with the help of the special needs department, designed to provide readily accessibly material suited to the needs of pupils with a range of needs.

Psychologists use the term 'locus of control' to refer to an individual's sense of control over his own environment. In the successful schools we studied, locus of control seemed to be centred firmly on the teacher. In other words, teachers generally accepted responsibility for what happened in their classrooms, and did not expect to refer pupils to colleagues at middle or senior management level. This sense of professional responsibility could not, however, have been achieved without a highly effective network of professional support.

The network operated at several levels. In one school every teacher had a list indicating where senior colleagues would be teaching at any given time. Faced with a discipline problem which seemed likely to escalate, a teacher could simply send a pupil to the class of a teacher on the list. The senior teacher would accept the child without comment, and with minimal interruption to his own lesson. At the end of the lesson the child would return to the original teacher. The aim was to 'defuse' a situation before it became serious, without removing responsibility from the teacher concerned. Later, the teacher might decide to seek support from senior colleagues in the pastoral network, such as the school counsellor or head of year, or from members of the special education department. That, however, would be his responsibility.

For newly qualified teachers, the induction process aimed to ensure that they knew where to turn for support, and encouraged openness in sharing, and solving, problems. One aspect of the induction process was a weekly meeting with the head to discuss professional issues arising in their first year of teaching. The fact that the head made time for this meeting illustrated the priority placed on teacher support in this school.

Staff Development

It was striking that in some schools many teachers seemed to regard senior colleagues as a source of criticism rather than of support. In others, such as the school described above, the reverse was the case. Perhaps the most important distinctions between the schools we studied were the priority they placed on staff development and on their success in providing opportunity for it.

This has seldom been more important than in the mid 1980s. L.e.a. money for in-service education is being cut, and the falling birth-rate, combined with the international economic climate, is leading to large numbers of school closures. Teachers can no longer expect regular promotion. Fewer vacancies result in greater stability of staffing. They can also result in many teachers becoming frustrated and resentful, feeling with some reason that society is neither valuing nor recognising their experience or enthusiasm. We have argued that one aim for teachers should be to enhance children's self-esteem, and to help them acquire a sense of developing competence. These needs are just as important for teachers. School effectiveness in general, and the education of children with special needs in particular, may depend largely on teachers feeling that they are acquiring new and useful skills. In this section we consider issues of staff development, with particular reference to staff with pastoral responsibilities, heads of special needs departments, and senior management.

Staff with Pastoral Responsibilities

The briefest analysis of a year tutor's job indicates the central importance of team leadership. It also indicates how easily this can be overlooked. A source of stress for many year tutors is knowing that they could tackle something more effectively than any member of their team of form tutors. Similar situations arise in primary schools. The temptation, sometimes almost irresistible, is to intervene oneself, or to accept personal responsibility for a child with special needs.

Yet as Marland (1983) points out, an effective pastoral network requires an effective team of form tutors. The head might be a better lower school English teacher than anyone in the English department. This does not mean that he should take lower school English classes himself. Rather it implies that he should find ways to improve the standard in the English department. Similarly, the head of year's task is the professional development of the form tutor team. This does not mean that he deals with no children individually. To command confidence a staff support network requires that action can be taken swiftly and decisively by senior members of staff. It does, however, mean that in dealing with children individually he retains a clear idea of the role and responsibilities of the form tutor and of subject teachers.

A common source of confusion when considering the staff development responsibilities of year tutors is a false analysis of what they can and cannot achieve. At in-service sessions they frequently complain, not always without justification: 'you should be talking to head teachers! *We* can't change the system!' Certainly, pastoral staff at middle management level cannot easily change the way their school organises pastoral care, at least in the short term, however open the head and deputies may be to suggestions for reorganisation in the future.

They do nevertheless have a great deal of scope. In most schools they are able to exert considerable influence over the use of tutorial time. The tutorial programme can be used as a way of getting through administrative choices. It can contain a 'mish-mash' of topics selected according to the whim of each form tutor. Alternatively, it can act as the focal point of a carefully planned pastoral programme. It is not desirable that form tutors should each plan a separate tutorial programme with their team of tutors. Some consistent themes are needed, to reflect the school's overall policy and to ensure development of content and conceptual level from year to year.

Implementing the tutorial programme, though, as well as detailed planning, offers enormous possibilities. Its success, and hence the satisfaction which both pupils and form tutors derive from it, depends largely on the year tutor's ability as leader of the tutorial team. Rutter *et al.* (1979) noted that joint curriculum planning characterised their more successful schools. In the less successful schools, teachers had greater individual discretion over curriculum content and materials. It seems logical that co-operative planning, with an emphasis on responsibility as members of a team would be of similar benefit in the pastoral network.

A co-ordinated tutorial programme extends a long way beyond the form tutor periods. It also enables the year tutor to keep in touch with form tutors and to monitor their work with individuals who may have special needs. Quite rightly, form tutors and pastoral staff frequently receive confidential information, from children, from parents and from other professionals. Particularly when they lack experience, for example because they are new to the profession, form tutors should not be expected to know how to use such information to the child's best advantage. Questions such as how much information should be passed on, to whom, for what purposes and when are all matters requiring discussion. Here too year tutors have important staff development responsibilities. Their job is not, in general, to deal with such issues themselves, but to ensure that members of their team acquire the knowledge, understanding and skill to deal with them sensitively and appropriately.

In our research in New Zealand we found that many teachers regarded interviews with parents as a source of substantial stress. Few primary heads or secondary school year tutors appear to see it as their job to help colleagues acquire skill and confidence in discussions with parents. One wonders why not. Lip service has been paid for years to the notion of parents as partners, especially with respect to children who have special needs. Many teachers gradually develop confidence in contacts with parents through a highly stressful process of trial and error. Yet this is a central aspect of the staff development responsibilities of senior members of pastoral teams, of equal importance in secondary and in primary schools.

Clearly, these suggestions carry implications for the training and professional development of pastoral staff themselves. They need leadership skills, and the ability to plan a tutorial programme with a team of colleagues, or at least to develop one from a broad outline. They also need the ability to work successfully with parents and with individual children in order to help and support their colleagues in such work. Pastoral staff, then, are dependent for their own professional development on the school's senior management. The same, of course, applies to teachers with responsibility for children with special needs.

Teachers in 'Special Needs' Departments

One theme throughout this book has been that teachers can cater successfully in ordinary schools for children with special needs. Another has been that this will seldom be achieved if the children are taught in self-contained special groups, or even if they are withdrawn from substantial parts of the 'ordinary' curriculum. It is extremely difficult, if not impossible, to prevent a full-time remedial class degenerating into a convenient receptacle for children that nobody else wants to teach. A policy of integrating children with special needs into ordinary classes carries obvious implications for teachers in ordinary classes. The implications for the skills needed by teachers in a special needs department are no less far-reaching, if somewhat less obvious.

The first implication is that much of the specialist teacher's work will be with colleagues, and not in direct work with the children themselves. Even when the specialist is working directly with a child, this may take place within an ordinary lesson, providing help which enables the child to benefit from the mainstream curriculum. It follows that the primary skill required by a teacher with responsibility for special needs is in working successfully with colleagues throughout the school.

A corollary of this argument is that the specialist's primary task is in the area of staff development, helping colleagues to acquire the skills to teach children with special needs. Our argument is not that all teachers should be specialists in children with special needs. We are, however, arguing that specialists should act as facilitators in helping teachers to adapt the curriculum in the light of the children's needs. Specialists act as providers of special education only in the indirect sense that they can provide or prepare materials which class teachers can utilise.

This role is not necessarily inconsistent with temporarily withdrawing children from ordinary class for some particular purpose. The value of intensive help in a small group will be reduced, though, if not altogether negated, if its content does not relate closely to what is being taught in the regular class. Discussing a behavioural objectives approach to the curriculum of children with special needs, Strivens (1981) argues that integration is inhibited precisely by the specialised nature of the programme.

Yet co-ordinating provision of special help in a withdrawal group with the regular curriculum is not a one-sided matter. It requires the specialist to adapt to the needs of the class or subject teachers. It also requires adaptation on the latter's part. That is only likely to be achieved when they feel not only that the programme may benefit the child, but also that it enhances their own knowledge and understanding. This is not unrealistic. Most teachers derive great satisfaction from seeing a child with special needs make progress. More important, perhaps, their work with such children generally enhances their professional ability, with benefit to many other children in the class

An integration policy also carries important implications for assessment. Heads of special needs departments sometimes have quite extensive knowledge and experience in assessment techniques. They may be skilled in using the results to plan individual remedial programmes. These may be of limited value, though, when the aim is to provide special educational help in the mainstream. The emphasis then is on applying information from assessment, based on observation as well as more formal techniques, in the classroom. This too has implications for staff development. Too often educational psychologists and specialist teachers spend a lot of time and energy carrying out detailed, extensive investigations when information much closer to hand is not being utilised. The reason frequently, for not using it lies in class and subject teachers not recognising its significance or not knowing how to apply it in their work with the child.

Head Teachers and Senior Management

The head teacher's influence on school climate and on the lives both of teachers and of pupils is not in dispute. Without a clear policy from the head, provision for children with special needs inevitably becomes haphazard and unco-ordinated. Management courses for head teachers have become an established part of the education scene in Britain and elsewhere. There is remarkably little research, though, on how head teachers affect school climate, and even less on the sort of training from which they might benefit.

Research in industry suggests that white collar workers experience stress from an excessive work-load, job complexity and responsibility for employees. Blue collar workers, in contrast, feel stress because their abilities are under-utilised, and from lack of complexity in their jobs (Cooper, 1980). Translating these observations into schools, heads and senior staff may engender stress for themselves by inability to delegate responsibility. Looking at the number and scope of their responsibilities the stress is not surprising. At the same time they may generate stress for their junior colleagues who feel frustrated and under-valued, and may resent the administrative inefficiency resulting from failure to delegate.

An American study has suggested that younger school administrators might benefit from training in how to manage their time effectively, while older administrators may need courses in interpersonal skills (Tung and Koch, 1980). There is no doubt about the complexity of the job (e.g. Wolcott, 1973; Vetter, 1976; Edwards, 1979). One aspect of this is the possible conflict between enjoyment in working with children or with staff, and the routine administrative responsibilities of the job (e.g. Isherwood and Tallboy, 1979).

Primary head teachers in New Zealand consistently referred to administrative tasks and interpersonal relationships with colleagues as their major sources of stress. Further analysis showed that stress increased when the school served a socially disadvantaged catchment area, the school buildings were inadequate and, interestingly, the head did not have responsibility for a class. We suggested that heads who did not have regular classroom responsibility might experience more conflict between their role as teachers and as administrators. In addition, the 'help' which they offered colleagues could readily be interpreted by the colleagues as interference (Galloway *et al.*, 1982*b*, *c*).

Two further indications emerged from the study. First, heads who were undertaking advanced studies in education, for example part-time university courses, tended to report less stress than other head teachers. Second, heads who said they received substantial help from parents reported less stress than heads who said they only received some help, or little to none. These differences could not be attributed to the school's catchment areas. The implications may be trite, but they are at least logical. First, heads who take their own professional development seriously may be better equipped to promote that of their colleagues. Second, heads who succeed in establishing good relationships with parents may not only provide a valuable model to enhance their colleagues' professional development, but also derive personal benefits.

Class teachers in the New Zealand study reported significantly greater job-satisfaction if their head teacher was aged less than 50 than when he was aged 50 or over (Galloway *et al.*, 1985). While this observation tends to strengthen Tung and Koch's (1980) view that older administrators may need courses in staff management, it tells us nothing about the management styles which promote job satisfaction. In our study of four schools with low rates of disruptive behaviour, we regarded one head's style as democratic, two as autocratic and one as mixed. There was, however, one common element:

> Irrespective of style, leadership in all four schools was strong and accepted. The head teacher communicated his philosophy and goals to teachers, and through them to pupils and to the community. Teachers mostly felt that their problems were understood, and their efforts and achievements respected. Decisions might be autocratic, but they were not arbitrary (Galloway, 1983, p. 252).

This view is consistent with an earlier suggestion by Nias (1980). Interviews with newly qualified graduate primary teachers suggested strong dissatisfaction both when the head's leadership style was passive and when it was 'characterised by social distance, authoritarian professional relationships and administrative inefficiency'. 'Positive' leadership, on the other hand, implied high professional standards, consultation with colleagues, and active support for their professional development. Having positive leadership was not in itself a source of satisfaction for teachers. It did, however, promote job satisfaction by providing a climate which facilitated successful work in the classroom and co-operative relationships with colleagues.

Conclusions and Summary

This chapter has focused on a neglected aspect of special educational needs, namely the effect of the school's climate on its teachers as well as on its pupils. Thus, much of the chapter has drawn on material which was not originally seen as contributing to the debate about special needs. There is no doubt, however, that children with special needs are the focus for a great deal of stress experienced by their teachers. Nor is there the slightest doubt that teachers who are dissatisfied and feeling the effects of excessive stress may particularly resent the added challenge presented by pupils with special needs.

Obedience to the letter of the 1981 Education Act is a matter of attention to bureaucratic detail. If the spirit of the Act is also to be implemented there will be far reaching changes in the policy and organisation of schools. These changes will affect all teachers. Potentially, they could generate a lot of extra stress. They could also lead to greatly enhanced job satisfaction. They affect the school's emotional climate as much as its academic curriculum. A school's success in implementing the Act may depend on its success in furthering the professional development of its own staff.

8 CONCLUSIONS: CREATING SPECIAL EDUCATIONAL NEEDS? OR MEETING THEM?

Overview

Warnock's conclusion that up to 20 per cent of pupils may present evidence of special educational needs at some stage in their school career has not been seriously questioned. Objectors may legitimately argue that the manner in which educational tests, developmental schedules and behaviour screening instruments are constructed ensures that results will identify a 'backward' or 'deviant' minority. The size of this minority then becomes a matter for debate, but the ultimate decision is an arbitrary one: individual researchers, or a committee of the Great and the Good have to make a moral and political judgement by defining a cut-off point at which a child should be regarded as having a problem or in the current terminology, as having special needs.

For most of the pupils we have been discussing in this book, special need is defined for the first time at school. The evidence, for the majority, is lack of educational progress or problems of personal or social adjustment. There are two senses in which attention to these pupils is timely. Their needs can all too easily be subordinated to those of more academic pupils. This has undoubtedly happened in the past and continues to occur at more than a few schools. Without attention they are unlikely to derive from their schooling the benefits which they themselves, their parents and teachers are entitled to expect. They constitute a substantial and continuing source of stress for teachers, and frequently become the focus for discontent which is not of their own making.

It is noteworthy, then, that needs which are identified in school may also be aggravated, if not created, within the school. Children who have presented enormous learning and behavioural problems with one teacher can settle happily with another teacher and start to make good progress. The same can occur following a change of school. General educational standards certainly reflect a school's catchment area to some extent. Nevertheless the chronic underachievement in some schools, which Warnock legitimately regarded as evidence of special educational needs, is not always reflected in neighbouring schools serving identical catchment areas. The amount of disturbing pupil behaviour, moreover, seems to depend much more on factors within the school than in the catchment area.

Important changes may take place in the curriculum, organisation and management of schools, ranging from the ILEA (1984) proposals for 'Improving Secondary Schools' to the DES (1984) proposed reform of school governing bodies. Many of these changes may benefit children with special needs. It seems almost certain, though, that differences between schools will remain as wide as ever. It also seems probable that differences within schools will remain as wide as ever. School effectiveness research suggests strongly that some schools succeed in raising the overall level of pupil performance. There is little evidence that schools can reduce differences in performance between pupils.

The implication is that it will be as easy to identify 16 – 20 per cent of pupils with special needs at the most successful school as at the least successful. The needs identified will almost certainly differ. For example, one would expect to find far fewer behaviour problems at successful schools. Further, the cut-off point by comparison with national norms would vary from school to school. The essential point, though, remains that a minority of pupils at each school will present problems by comparison with their educationally successful or socially more co-operative peers. Whether children are said to have special needs, then, depends as much on the standards of the majority as of the 'special' pupils themselves.

It follows that each school requires its own carefully planned policy towards children with special needs. Moreover, the policy will affect the work of all teachers and the education of all pupils in the school, irrespective of its nature. We have mentioned possibilities which illustrate this point. Children with special needs can, for example, be taught in a full-time class, separate from the mainstream. Whatever special class or remedial teachers may intend, their pupils will be in little doubt about their status in the school. Nor will pupils in ordinary classes entertain any doubts about the special pupils' status. For teachers of ordinary classes the questions in relation to any particular pupil are not whether he has special needs, and if so how they can be met, but rather whether he is 'bad enough' to warrant placement in the special class. Thus, the special class creates a hidden curriculum which affects pupils and teachers.

The second possibility is that children with special needs are, in general, taught in ordinary classes, with additional help and support available from specialist teachers. This too carries dangers. The policy may not be generally accepted by teachers, perhaps because of lack of specialist support, inter-departmental rivalry or generally low morale. It may then become the focus for discontent which affects adversely the education of all pupils. On the other hand it carries considerable possibilities. Working with colleagues to meet a child's needs is potentially a source of great satisfaction. Teachers rightly pride themselves on their professional competence. An opportunity, through membership of a team, to extend their understanding of special needs, and hence work successfully with a wider range of children, has personal as well as professional benefits.

Policy within schools, though, is influenced by national guidelines and by the l.e.a.'s own policy towards special needs. In this chapter we consider possible policy implications for the DES, l.e.a. administration, l.e.a. support services and individual schools. Finally, we return to the question of responsibility for children with special needs, arguing that the available evidence should make teachers cautiously optimistic about their ability to meet them.

DES and HMI Policy

The Inspectorate acts as 'the eyes and ears of the Department', but is technically independent of it. In recent years there has in fact been a good deal of tension between the Inspectorate and the Department, particularly when HMI has produced reports illustrating deteriorating physical and material standards in schools. Hence, it does not follow that published statements by HMI will necessarily receive the enthusiastic support of the Secretary of State and his Departmental officers.

While individual members of HMI appear, at least privately, to recognise the anomalies created by parallel systems of special and ordinary schools, it is not clear that they are recognised by civil servants in the DES. One problem lies in the divisive salary structure which pays a special schools allowance to teachers in recognised special schools or classes, but not to teachers in ordinary schools, even if they are better qualified. This discourages special school teachers from returning to the mainstream. It can also discourage teachers in the mainstream from taking extra qualifications.

Just as seriously, the parallel systems encourage a 'hidden agenda' when children are referred to educational psychologists. The formality of the 1981 Education Act's procedures makes this hidden agenda all the more obstructive. In theory, teachers refer children for advice on their needs. In theory, psychologists assess their needs without being influenced by the local availability of resources. In reality, teachers often want to know whether the child should be placed in the special system. Since, under current DES guidelines, formal statements are only required for children admitted to recognised special schools or classes, the possibility of transfer is bound to be prominent during the assessment process.

A third problem perpetuated by the parallel system is the illusion that special schools necessarily provide 'special' education. The evidence, overwhelmingly, is that they are if anything less successful in providing genuinely special education than ordinary schools. Research has consistently shown, for example, that ESN(M) pupils make better educational progress in ordinary schools.

Regrettably, the 1981 Act does little to encourage a range of l.e.a. policies that might break down the divisive parallel system. On the contrary it entrenches the system in at least two ways. First, transfer out of special schools is made more difficult than was previously the case. Second, special schools can only be closed with the Secretary of State's approval. This may be necessary to prevent local councillors making children with special needs the target of cost cutting exercises. The DES could nevertheless do much to encourage more imaginative solutions than simply maintaining the status quo.

Existing special schools might, for example, be developed as resource centres for teachers from surrounding primary and secondary schools. Alternatively they might offer an assessment service with intensive short-term help for small groups of children. If they offered short-term help they would have to work closely with local schools over the question of pupils' admission and of their return. This might enable them to develop as centres of excellence, playing a central part in the l.e.a.'s in-service education programme for teachers. Sadly, there are few indications that many special school teachers would welcome encouragement to extend their role in this way, nor that they could command much credibility from their ordinary school colleagues if they tried to do so.

Lacking a clear lead, either from legislation or from the

Secretary of State, HMI's scope for encouraging innovation is inevitably restricted. The inspectorate's influence through informal visits, through its periodic surveys and through its formal inspections both of l.e.a.'s and of individual schools, should not, however, be underestimated. Provision for children with special needs now receives attention in all major inspections. The inspectors do not hesitate to praise what they see as good practice nor to draw attention to deficiencies. Perhaps one measure of HMI's influence may be the development of co-ordinated policies towards special educational needs within l.e.a.s as well as within individual schools.

LEA Administration

Generous advisory and support services are a necessary aspect of l.e.a. policy towards children with special needs. Governors and head teachers cannot sensibly be expected to take these children's needs seriously if the l.e.a. itself does not. Generous advisory and support services are not, however, sufficient unless they operate within a logical, consistent framework. Head teachers cannot be expected to take much trouble over policy towards children with special needs if the l.e.a. administration manifestly fails to do so.

The bureaucratic requirements of the 1981 Act seem likely, as we have argued, to entrench the division between the ordinary and the special school systems. This need not happen. Much of the detail can be dealt with at clerical level. Nevertheless, the cumbersome machinery for special school entry and discharge, inevitable in the required Statement and re-assessment procedures, militates against an integrated system.

Since the legislative framework promotes divisions, it becomes all the more important for the l.e.a.'s administration to bridge the gap which legislation has perpetuated. With some notable exceptions, few l.e.a.s have responded to this challenge. Children with special needs do not, as the Warnock Report has forcefully pointed out, fall into any tidy administrative areas. It follows that administrative responsibility also crosses traditional boundaries. Thus, the sphere of the education officer with responsibility for special needs overlaps with that of the officer for primary schools and for secondary schools. In most l.e.a.'s the education officer for special needs has lower status than his primary and secondary colleagues, for example assistant education officer as opposed to senior assistant educational officer. It is hard to see how an l.e.a. can develop a co-ordinated policy, bridging the gap between special and ordinary schools, and promoting provision for children with special needs in the latter, when special education remains a relatively low status responsibility at administration level.

LEA Support Services

The activities of advisers also reflect confusion in l.e.a. policy towards special needs. In theory, advisers on special needs in most l.e.a.s divide their time between ordinary schools and special schools. In practice administrative constraints often combine with their own preferences to ensure that more of their time is spent in the latter. It is right that special schools should receive advisory support. Yet more than 90 per cent of children with special needs remain in ordinary schools. They, and their teachers, also merit support.

It is a truism that advice is useful only if accepted. Educational psychologists may carry out highly perceptive assessments and make wholly appropriate recommendations. Advisers and advisory teachers may be similarly perceptive. Whatever the quality of the advice they proffer, it will be of no practical value to teachers, or to children, unless teachers are willing to try to implement it. Thus, the success of advisory services depends on the individual adviser or psychologist establishing a co-operative relationship with teachers. It follows that their work must be as much with teachers as with children. For advisers this is uncontroversial. Nor would most educational psychologists see anything controversial here. Yet the procedures of the 1981 Act, with their heavy emphasis on individual assessments, will reduce the time they can spend with teachers. In other words they will become more concerned with assessing special needs than with meeting them.

The architects of the Act implicitly recognised this danger, and tried to circumvent it. The major purpose of assessment, according to the DES (1983) guidelines, is to prescribe rather than to diagnose. The statement should indicate not only the nature of a child's needs, but also how they should be met. Annual reviews should ensure that no child is left to founder in the system. Whether the aims of the Act are reflected in professional practice remains to be seen. Grounds for concern are nevertheless evident. It is not clear how many children in ordinary schools will have the 'protection' of a statement under the Act. In some l.e.a.'s, such as Oxfordshire, only children placed in special schools or classes will receive Statements. Even when a child is, in the new jargon, 'Statemented' it is doubtful whether a psychologist or adviser will be able to spend much time helping a teacher to implement recommendations from the assessment.

The reason, at least for educational psychologists, is that they face two major constraints. One lies in the continually pressing need to deal with new referrals. The second lies in recognition that an individual's needs must be met in the classroom, frequently by teachers who lack any special training. Consequently, suggestions for meeting an individual child's needs may have not the slightest value until more fundamental issues of classroom management have been tackled. In theory, advisers tackle such issues. In practice, assessment and subsequent planning cannot be divorced from the school and classroom context in which the child's needs are identified and met.

Educational psychologists, and to a lesser extent advisers and advisory teachers, face a conflict between loyalty to their child clients and to their teacher colleagues. There is inevitable tension between describing the child's needs and suggestions on how these should be met. The tension arises because the description may contain implicit criticism of the school or of particular teachers, leading to unwilling acquiescence in subsequent plans for the child if not to outright rejection. This tension is increased by the parallel system since transfer to a special school can only be interpreted, with relief or resentment, as an indication of the ordinary school's inability to cater for the child.

This tension is probably not avoidable, but is greatly reduced when members of the support services succeed in establishing a working partnership with teachers. The question then is not where the child's needs should be met, but rather what additional resources or curriculum changes are needed to meet them in the referring school. With this approach, the support services become more accountable to teachers, since they are involved in planning and implementing their own recommendations. It does, however, require that all the support services recognise that their responsibility lies as much in working with teachers as with children, and that the l.e.a.'s acceptance of this principle is recognised in staffing levels.

Schools

At local authority level, policy is influenced by political as well as educational considerations. Whether an l.e.a. adopts a formal stance on such diverse issues as mixed ability teaching, corporal punishment and special educational needs depends as much on the political complexion and bias of its education committee members as on the interests and energy of the chief education officer and his senior colleagues. L.e.a. policy is not, however, necessarily reflected in school practice. Teachers in Britain, especially head teachers, have greater automomy than in most countries. L.e.a.s cannot easily compel their schools to adopt a particular policy towards special needs. An l.e.a. can encourage schools to make adequate provision for pupils with special needs in a number of ways. They can provide additional resources. They can restrict the number of special school places, though the Secretary of State's permission must be obtained before closing a special school. They can encourage the use of formal procedures leading to Statements under the 1981 Act on behalf of children in ordinary schools, with the consequent obligation on governing bodies to review the children's progress.

Yet these are pretty peripheral measures. Their impact on what schools actually offer the pupils concerned can easily be minimal. Schools which wish to ignore the spirit of the Act while conforming to its detailed requirements may find it convenient to place children with Statements in separate classes, releasing them for token integration in subjects such as PE which are considered relatively unimportant. L.e.a. policy can and should encourage a wider concept of special education. Ultimately, though, the quality of children's experience at school depends on their teachers.

Accepting the prevalence, range and complexity of special needs entails radical re-thinking of policy and practice throughout the school. In the past many heads took pride in remedial departments operating as self-contained classes, perhaps with the additional possibility of temporarily withdrawing some pupils for special help in particular areas. Such departments were sometimes generously staffed by able and sympathetic teachers. They suffered, though, from a number of problems.

They could not easily avoid becoming a receptacle for children no-one else wanted to teach. Transfer in and out of the mainstream was difficult to arrange. They were insufficiently flexible to cater for children in the mainstream whose special needs did not fit neatly into one of the existing withdrawal groups or who did not require a full-time class. In consequence, they were of little relevance or practical help to teachers in the mainstream.

Children with special needs may be found in *all* classes in a school. An average primary school or mixed ability secondary school class may contain at least five or six children with special needs. The higher ability classes of banded or streamed secondary schools will also contain children with special needs, though in smaller number than the lower ability classes, and with different problems. It follows that staff development is an essential aspect of a school's provision for children with special needs. A different way of saying the same thing is that a school cannot take its children's needs seriously without also meeting the needs of its teachers.

A school's success in this respect depends partly on the consistency and clarity of the head's philosophy that recognising and meeting special needs is every teacher's responsibility. It also depends on general acceptance of this philosophy. Head teachers can facilitate or inhibit professional development of their senior colleagues. In their turn, teachers with responsibility for pastoral care and heads of departments of special needs can facilitate or inhibit their colleagues' professional development. Teachers who feel that their own needs are being met are likely to derive high job satisfaction and to find the energy to devote extra time and attention to children with special needs. The reverse is equally true.

Whose Responsibility?

We have talked consistently about children with special needs, but their needs must be seen, at least in part, as the product of their environment at home and at school. We do not deny for a moment the importance of factors within the child or within the family in the origin of many children's special needs. An aim of this book, however, has been to insist that the school is of equal importance. An intellectually dull child from a grossly stressful background may be able to tolerate the stress at home if he feels he is achieving something worthwhile at school and that his teachers recognise and value his achievements. If this child's self-image is further damaged by consistent failure at school, with no prospect for the future except further failure and frustration, teachers and society may well find they have a problem on their hands. In assessing the child's special needs it will be tempting to attribute responsibility to the family when other solutions lie closer to hand.

The competence of teachers is not enhanced by passing responsibility for children with special needs to educational psychologists or to colleagues in special schools. Nor is their self-esteem. Yet either alternative is preferable to the feeling of helplessness produced by inaction while children's needs grow more and more acute.

Satisfaction from teaching depends heavily on the intrinsic aspects of the job, such as establishing co-operative relationships with children and seeing them make progress. When working with children who have special needs, the challenge is greater, but so are the rewards. No teacher can expect to work successfully with such childen without support, both from colleagues and from the l.e.a.'s support services. The stated aim may be to help the child, but an equally important function will be to give the teacher greater confidence and enhanced job satisfaction.

To conclude, the evidence suggests that children's behaviour and progress at school is strongly influenced by the quality of their experience at school. The evidence can be interpreted in two ways. One argument is that some schools successfully meet the needs of children who would be considered a much more serious problem at others. With respect to educationally backward children this is certainly the case. The second argument is that some schools succeed in creating a social climate in which the question seldom arises of children's disturbing behaviour being taken as evidence of them having special needs. In some schools, where disruptive behaviour appears to be a relatively minor problem, this also appears to be the case. In either case the message is an encouraging one: that schools can cater successfully for their most vulnerable children.

REFERENCES

Anderson, E. (1973) *The Disabled Schoolchild: A Study of Integration in Primary Schools*, Methuen, London.

Archer, W.N. (1973) *A Study of the Effects of a Remedial Teaching Programme for Maladjusted Children in Normal Primary Schools*, Unpublished Dissertation for University of London Diploma in Education with Special Reference to Children up to the Age of Thirteen Years. Maria Grey College, London.

Baldwin, J. (1972) 'Delinquent Schools in Tower Hamlets, 1, A Critique', *British Journal of Criminology*, 12, 399 – 401.

Bandura, A. (1974) 'Behaviour Theory and Models of Man', *American Psychologist*, 29, 859 – 69.

Barker Lunn, J.C. (1970) *Streaming in the Primary School*, NFER, Windsor.

Barton, L. and Moody, M. (1981) 'The Value of Parents to the ESN(S) School: An Examination', In L. Barton and S. Tomlinson (eds.), *Special Education: Policy, Practices and Social Issues*, Harper and Row, London.

Barton, L. and Tomlinson, S. (1981) *Special Education: Policy, Practices and Social Issues*, Harper and Row, London.

Bennett, N. (1976) *Teaching Styles and Pupil Progress*, Open Books, London.

Beresford, P., Booth, T., Croft, S. and Tuckwell, P. (1983) 'An ESN(S) School and the Labour Market', In T. Booth and J. Statham (eds.), *The Nature of Special Education*, Croom Helm, London.

Berger, M. (1979) 'Behaviour Modification in Education and Professional Practice: The Dangers of a Mindless Technology', *Bulletin of the British Psychological Society*, 32, 418 – 19.

Berger, M. (1982) 'Applied Behaviour Analysis in Education: A Critical Assessment and Some Implications for Training Teachers', *Educational Psychology*, 2, 289 – 300.

Bernstein, B. (1971) *Class, Codes and Control, Vol. I. Theoretical Studies Towards a Sociology of Language*, Routledge and Kegan Paul, London.

Best, R., Jarvis, C.B. and Ribbins, P.M. (1977) Pastoral Care: Concept and Process, *British Journal of Educational Studies*, 25, 124 – 35.

Best, R., Ribbins, P., Jarvis, C. with Oddy, D. (1983) *Education and Care*, Heinemann, London.

Board of Education and Board of Control (1929) *Report of the Joint Departmental Committee on Mental Deficiency*, HMSO, London.

Bolger, A.W. (1983) 'Training in Counselling', British Psychological Society, *Education Section Review*, 7, ii, 33 – 8.

Booth, T. (1983) 'Creating Integration Policy', In T. Booth and P. Potts (eds.), *Integrating Special Education*, Blackwell, Oxford.

Booth, T. and Potts, P. (1983) *Creating Integration Policy*, Blackwell, Oxford.

Booth, T. and Statham, J. (1982) *The Nature of Special Education*, Croom Helm, London.

Bower, G.H. and Hilgard, E.R. (1981) *Theories of Learning*, Prentice Hall, New Jersey.

Boxall, M. (1973) 'Nurture Groups', *Concern*, 13, 9 – 11

Bryans, T. and Wolfendale, S. (1973) *Guide-lines for Teachers*, Reading and Language Development Centre, Croydon

Burt, C. (1937) *The Backward Child*, Hodder and Stoughton, London

Cantwell, D. (1977) 'Hyperkinetic Syndrome', In M. Rutter and L. Hersov (eds.), *Child Psychiatry: Modern Approaches*, Blackwell, Oxford

Carlberg, C. and Kavale, K. (1980) 'Efficacy of Special versus Regular Class Placement for Exceptional Children: A Meta-Analysis', *Journal of Special Education*, 14, 295 – 309

Cashdan, A. and Pumphrey, P.D. (1969) Some Effects of the Remedial Teaching of Reading, *Educational Research*, 11, 138 – 42

Clark, M.M. (1979) Why Remedial? Implications of Using the Concept of Remedial Education. In C. Gains and J.A. McNicholas (eds.), *Guidelines for the Future*, Longman, London

Clark, R.V.G. and Cornish, D.B. (1978) 'The Effectiveness of Residential Treatment for Delinquents', In L. Hersov, M. Berger and D. Schaffer (eds.), *Aggression and Anti-Social Behaviour in Childhood and Adolescence*, Pergamon, Oxford

Clunies-Ross, L. and Reid, M.J. (1980) *Mixed Ability Teaching: An Exploration of Teacher's Aims, Objectives and Classroom Strategies*, (Mimeograph report) NFER, Windsor

Coard, B. (1971) *How the West Indian Child is Made Educationally Subnormal in the British School System*, New Beacon Books, London

Coates, T.J. and Thoresen, C.E. (1976) 'Teacher Anxiety: A Review with Recommendations' *Review of Educational Research*, 46, 159 – 84

Cohen, L. and Fisher, D. (1973) 'Are Comprehensive Aims Being Realised?', *Journal of Curriculum Studies*, 5, 166 – 75

Coleman, J.S. *et al* (1966) *Equality of Educational Opportunity*, US Government Printing Office, Washington

Cooper, C.L. (1980) Work Stress in White- and Blue-Collar Jobs, *Bulletin of the British Psychological Society*, 33, 49 – 51

Cope, C. and Anderson, E. (1977) *Special Units in Ordinary Schools: An Exploratory Study of Special Provision for Disabled Children*, University of London Institute of Education, London

Corrigan, P. (1979) *Schooling the Smash Street Kids*, Macmillan, London

Cox, K.M. and Lavelle, M. (1982) *Staff Development Through Teacher Interaction: A School-Based Case Study*, Sheffield City Polytechnic, Department of Educational Management, Sheffield

Cox, T. (1978) *Stress*, Macmillan, London

Dain, P. (1977) Disruptive Children and the Key Centre, *Remedial Education*, 12, iv, 163 – 7

Daniels, J.C. and Diack, H. (1958) *The Standard Reading Tests*, Chatto and Windus, London

Davie, R., Butler, N. and Goldstein, H. (1972) *From Birth to Seven*, Longmans, London

Department of Education and Science (1967) *Children and Their Primary Schools* (The Plowden Report), HMSO, London

Department of Education and Science (1972) *Children with Specific Reading Difficulties: Report of the Advisory Committee on Handicapped Children*,

HMSO, London

Department of Education and Science (1975) *The Discovery of Children Requiring Special Education and the Assessment of Their Needs*, Circular 2/75, DES, London

Department of Education and Science (1976) *A Language for Life* (The Bullock Report), HMSO, London

Department of Education and Science (1978*a*) *Special Educational Needs* (The Warnock Report), HMSO, London

Department of Education and Science (1978*b*) *Mixed Ability Work in Comprehensive Schools*, HMSO, London

Department of Education and Science (1979) *Aspects of Secondary Education in England: A Survey by HM Inspectors of Schools*, HMSO, London

Department of Education and Science (1983) *Assessments and Statements of Special Educational Needs*, Circular 1/83, DES, London

Department of Education and Science (1984) *Parental Influence at School: A New Framework for School Government in England and Wales*, HMSO, London

Dessent, T. (1983) 'Who is Responsible for Children with Special Needs?' In T. Booth and P. Potts (eds.), *Integrating Special Education*, Blackwell, Oxford

Downey, M.E. (1977) *Interpersonal Judgements in Education*, Harper and Row, London

Dunham, J. (1976) 'Stress Situations and Responses', In National Association of Schoolmasters and Union of Women Teachers (eds.), *Stress in Schools*, NAS/UWT, Hemel Hempstead

Dunham, J. (1977) 'The Effects of Disruptive Behaviour on Teachers', *Educational Research*, 29, 181 – 7

Dunn, L.M. (1968) 'Special Education for the Mildly Retarded — is Much of it Justifiable?' *Exceptional Children*, 35, 5 – 22 (reprinted in W.G. Becker (ed.), An Empirical Basis for Change in Education, Science Research Associates, Henley-on-Thames

Dweck, C.S. (1977) 'Learned Helplessness and Negative Evaluation', *Education UCLA)*, 19, ii

Dyer, H.S. (1968) 'School Factors and Equal Educational Opportunity', *Harvard Educational Review*, 38, 38 – 56

Edelwich, J. and Brodsky, A. (1980) *Burn-out: Stages of Disillusionment in the Helping Professions*, Human Sciences Press, New York

Education Act (1944) 7 and 8 George VI, Ch. 31, HMSO, London

Education Act (1976) Elizabeth II, Ch. 81, HMSO, London

Education Act (1980) Elizabeth II, Ch. 20, HMSO, London

Education Act (1981) Elizabeth II, Ch. 60, HMSO, London

Edwards, W.L. (1979) 'The Role of the Principal in Five New Zealand Primary Schools: An Ethnographic Perspective', *Journal of Educational Administration*, 17, 248 – 54.

Farrington, D. (1972) 'Delinquency Begins at Home', *New Society*, 21, 14, September, 495 – 7

Ferguson, N. and Adams, M. (1982) 'Assessing the Advantages of Team Teaching in Remedial Education: The Remedial Teacher's Role', *Remedial Education*, 17, i, 24 – 30

Fitzherbert, K. (1977*a*) 'Unwillingly to School', *New Society*, 39, 17, February, 332 – 4.

Fitzherbert, K. (1977*b*) *Child Care Services and the Teacher*, Maurice Temple Smith, London

Ford, J. (1969) *Social Class and the Comprehensive School*, Routledge and Kegan Paul, London

Ford, J., Mungon, D. and Whelan, M. (1982) *Special Education and Social Control: Invisible Disasters*, Routledge and Kegan Paul, London

Frampton, O. (1981) *The Social Adjustment and Academic Achievement of Segregated and Integrated Slow-Learners in a Christchurch Secondary School*, University of Canterbury Education Department, Christchurch, New Zealand

Galloway, D. (1980) 'Exclusion from School', *Trends in Education*, ii, 33 – 8

Galloway, D. (1981) *Teaching and Counselling: Pastoral Care in Primary and Schools*, Longman, London

Galloway, D. (1982*a*) 'A Study of Persistent Absentees from School and their Families', *British Journal of Educational Psychology*, 52, 317 – 30

Galloway, D. (1982*b*) 'A Study of Pupils Suspended from School', *British Journal of Educational Psychology*, 52, 205 – 12

Galloway, D. (1982*c*) 'Deviance in Secondary Schools: A Question of Educational and Political Priorities for Educational Psychologists', *Occasional Papers, BPS Division of Educational and Child Psychology*, 6, iii, 7 – 13

Galloway, D. (1983) 'Disruptive Pupils and Effective Pastoral Care', *School Organisation*, 3, 245 – 54

Galloway, D. and Barrett, C. (1982) *Unmanageable Children? A Study of Recent Provision for Disruptive Pupils in the New Zealand Education System*, Victoria University of Wellington, Department of Education, Wellington

Galloway, D. and Barret, C. (1984) 'Off-site Centres for Disruptive Secondary School Pupils in New Zealand', *Educational Research*, 26, 106 – 10

Galloway, D. and Goodwin, C. (1979) *Educating Slow-Learning and Maladjusted Children: Integration or Segregation?* Longman, London

Galloway, D., Ball, T., Blomfield, D. and Seyd, R. (1982*a*) *Schools and Disruptive Pupils*, Longman, London

Galloway, D., Boswell, K., Panckhurst, F., Boswell, C. and Green, K. (1985) 'Sources of Satisfaction and Dissatisfaction for New Zealand Primary School Teachers', *Educational Research* (in press)

Galloway, D., Martin, R. and Wilcox, B. (1984*a*) 'Persistent Absence from School and Exclusion from School: The Predictive Power of School and Community Variables', *British Educational Research Journal* (in press)

Galloway, D. with Panckhurst, F. and Boswell, K. (1982*b*) *Teachers and Stress* Victoria University of Wellington Department of Education, Wellington

Galloway, D., Panckhurst, F., Boswell, C., Boswell, K. and Green, K. (1982*c*) 'Sources of Stress for Class Teachers', *National Education* (New Zealand), 64, 164 – 9

Galloway, D., Panckhurst, F., Boswell, K., Boswell, C. and Green, K. (1984*b*) 'Research Note: Mental Health, Absences from Work, Stress and Satisfaction in a Sample of New Zealand Primary School Teachers', *Australia and New Zealand Journal of Psychiatry* (in press)

Garnett, J. (1983) 'Providing Access to the Mainstream Curriculum in Secondary Schools', In T. Booth and P. Potts (eds.), *Integrating Special Education*, Blackwell, Oxford

Gath, D., Cooper, B. and Gattoni, F.E.G. (1972) 'Child Guidance and

Delinquency in a London Borough: Preliminary Communication', *Psychological Medicine*, 2, 185 – 91

Gath, D., Cooper, B., Gattoni, F. and Rockett, D. (1977) *Child Guidance and Delinquency in a London Borough*, Oxford University Press, Oxford

Gillham, B. (ed.) (1978) *Reconstructing Educational Psychology*, Croom Helm, London

Gillham, B. (1980) *Basic Number Diagnostic Test*, Hodder and Stoughton, London

Gillham, B. (1981) *Problem Behaviour in the Secondary School: A Systems Approach*, Croom Helm, London

Goodwin, C. (1983) 'The Contribution of Support Services to Integration Policy', In T. Booth and P. Potts (eds.), *Integrating Special Education*, Blackwell, Oxford

Gorrell-Barnes, G. (1973) 'Work with Nurture-Group Parents', *Concern*, 13, 13 – 16

Gregory, R.P. (1980) 'Individual Referrals: How Naive are Educational Psychologists?', *Bulletin of the British Psychological Society*, 33, 381 – 4

Gregson, A. and Quin, W.F. (1978) 'Mixed Ability Methods and Educational Standards', *Comprehensive Education*, 37, 12 – 16

Grunsell, R. (1978) *Born to be Invisible: The Story of a School for Truants*, Macmillan Education, London

Grunsell, R. (1979) Suspensions and the Sin-Bin Boom, *Where*, 153, 307 – 9

Grunsell, R. (1980) *Beyond Control? Schools and Suspension*, Readers and Writers, London

Haggerty, M.E. (1925) The Incidence of Undesirable Behaviour in Public-School Children, *Journal of Educational Research*, 12, 102 – 22

Haigh, G. (1975) *Pastoral Care*, Pitman, London

Hamblin, D. (1978) *The Teacher and Pastoral Care*, Blackwell, Oxford

Hargreaves, D.H. (1967) *Social Relationships in a Secondary School*, Routledge and Kegan Paul, London

Hargreaves, D.H. (1978) 'What Teaching Does to Teachers', *New Society*, 43, 9 March, 540 – 2

Hargreaves, D.H. (1983) *The Challenge of the Comprehensive School: Culture, Curriculum, Community*, Routledge and Kegan Paul, London

Harris, R. (1978) 'Relationships Between EEG Abnormality and Aggressive and Anti-Social Behaviour — A Critical Appraisal', in L.A. Hersov, M. Berger and D. Shaffer (eds.), *Aggression and Anti-Social Behaviour in Childhood and Adolescence*, Pergaman, Oxford

Harrop, L.A. (1980) 'Behaviour Modification in Schools: A Time for Caution', *Bulletin of the British Psychological Society*, 33, 158 – 60

Hegarty, S. and Pocklington, K. with Lucas, D. (1981) *Educating Pupils with Special Needs in the Ordinary School*, NFER/Nelson, Windsor

Hegarty, S. and Pocklington, K. with Lucas, D. (1982) *Integration in Action: Case Studies in the Integration of Pupils with Special Needs*, NFER/Nelson, Windsor

Her Majesty's Inspectorate of Schools (1978) *Behavioural Units*, DES, London

Herzberg, F., Mausner, B. and Snyderman, B.B. (1959) *The Motivation to Work*, 2nd edn, Wiley, New York

Hewison, J. and Tizard, J. (1980) 'Parental Involvement and Reading Attainment', *British Journal of Educational Psychology*, 50, 209 – 15

Holdaway, E.A. (1978) 'Facet and Overall Satisfaction of Teachers', *Educational Administration Quarterly*, 14, 30 – 47

Hood-Williams, J. (1960) 'The Results of Psychotherapy with Children: A Revaluation', *Journal of Consulting Psychology*, 24, 84 – 8

Inner London Education Authority (1984) *Improving Secondary Schools* (The Hargreaves Report), ILEA, London

Isherwood, G.B. and Tallboy, R.W. (1979) 'Reward Systems of Elementary School Principals: An Exploratory Study', *Journal of Educational Administration*, 17, 160 – 70

Jehu, D., Hardiker, P., Yelloly, M. and Shaw, M. (1972) *Behaviour Modification in Social Work*, Wiley-Interscience, London

Jencks, C. (1972) *Inequality: A Re-Assessment of the Effects of Family and Schooling in America*, Basic Books, New York

Jones, A. (1980) The School's View of Persistent Non-Attendance, in L. Hersov and I. Berg (eds.), *Out of School: Modern Perspectives in Truancy and School Refusal*, Wiley, Chichester

Jones, E. (1983) 'Resources for Meeting Special Needs in Ordinary Schools', in T. Booth and P. Potts (eds.), *Integrating Special Education*, Blackwell, Oxford

Jones, N. (1973) 'Special Adjustment Units in Comprehensive Schools: I Needs and Resources, II Structure and Function', *Therapeutic Education*, 1, ii, 23 – 31

Jones, N. (1974) 'Special Adjustment Units in Comprehensive Schools: III Selection of Children', *Therapeutic Education*, 2, ii, 21 – 6

Jones, N. (1983) 'The Management of Integration: The Oxfordshire Experience', in T. Booth and P. Potts (eds.), *Integrating Special Education*, Blackwell, Oxford

Kazdin, A.E. (1978) *History of Behaviour Modification*, University Park Press, Baltimore

Kligman, D. and Goldberg, D.A. (1975) 'Temporal Lobe Epilepsy and Aggression', *Journal of Nervous and Mental Disorder*, 160, 324 – 41

Kyriacou, C. and Sutcliffe, J. (1978) 'A Model of Teacher Stress', *Educational Studies*, 4, 1 – 6

Kyriacou, C. and Sutcliffe, J. (1979) 'Teacher Stress and Satisfaction', *Educational Research*, 21, 89 – 96

Labon, D. (1973) 'Helping Maladjusted Children in Primary Schools', *Therapeutic Education*, 1, 2, 14 – 22

Labon, D. (1974) 'Some Effects of School-Based Therapy', *Association of Educational Psychologists Journal*, 3, vi, 28 – 34

Labov, W. (1970) 'The Logic of Non-Standard English', in F. Williams (ed.), *Language and Poverty: Perspectives on a Theme*, Markham, Chicago

Landsman, L. (1978) 'Is Teaching Hazardous to Your Health', *Today's Education*, 67, 2, 48 – 50

Lane, D. (1977) 'Aspects of the Use of Behaviour Modification in Secondary Schools', *Bulletin of the British Association for Behavioural Psychotherapy*, 5, 76 – 9

Lansdown, R. (1978) 'Retardation in Mathematics: A Consideration of Multi-Factorial Determination', *Journal of Child Psychology and Psychiatry*, 19, 181 – 5

Lawler, E.E. (1973) *Motivation in Work Organisations*, Brooks/Cole, Monterey, California

Lawrence, J., Steed, D. and Young, P. (1977) *Disruptive Behaviour in a Secondary School*, Goldsmiths' College, University of London

Levitt, E.E. (1963) 'Psychotherapy with Children: A Further Evaluation', *Behavioural Research and Therapy*, 1, 45 – 51

Lindsay, G. (1982) *The Infant Rating Scale: Specimen Set*, Hodder and Stoughton, Sevenoaks

Lloyd-Smith, M. (1979) 'The Meaning of Special Units', *Socialism and Education*, 6, ii, 10 – 11

Local Government Training Board (1972) *Training of Educational Welfare Officers: Training Recommendation 19*, Local Government Training Board, Luton

McFie, B.S. (1934) 'Behaviour and Personality Difficulties in School Children', *British Journal of Educational Psychology*, 4, 30 – 46

Marland, M. (1974) *Pastoral Care*, Heinemann, London

Marland, M. (1980) 'The Pastoral Curriculum', in R. Best, C. Jarvis and P. Ribbins (eds.), *Perspectives in Pastoral Care*, Heinemann, London

Marland, M. (1983) Preparing for Promotion in Pastoral Care, *Pastoral Care in Education*, 1, 24 – 36

Milner, M. (1938) *The Human Problem in Schools*, Methuen, London

Ministry of Education (1945) *The Handicapped Pupils and School Health Service Regulations* (S.R. and O. No. 1076), HMSO, London

Ministry of Education (1958) *Report of the Chief Medical Officer for the Years 1956 – 57*, HMSO, London

Ministry of Education (1959) *The Handicapped Pupils and Special Schools Regulation*, (S.I. No. 365), HMSO, London

Ministry of Education (1961) *Special Educational Treatment for Educationally Sub-Normal Pupils*, Circular 11/61, Ministry of Education, London

Mitchell, S. and Rosa, P. (1981) 'Boyhood Behaviour Problems as Precursors of Criminality: A Fifteen Year Follow-Up', *Journal of Child Psychology and Psychiatry*, 22, 19 – 33

Mittler, P. (1978) 'Choices in Partnership', in *Lebenshilfe für Behinderte*, (ed.) World Congress in the ILSMH, on Medical Handicap

Murgatroyd, S. (1983) 'Counselling at a Time of Change and Development', British Psychological Society, *Education Section Review*, 7, ii, 5 – 9

Murphy, P.J. (1981) *The Ascertainment of Mild Subnormality in Education — A Case Study Approach*, unpublished Master's in Child Development Dissertation, University of London Institute of Education, London

Nash, R. (1978) *Teacher Expectations and Pupil Learning*, Routledge and Kegan Paul, London

Nash, R. (1983) 'Four Charges Against TOSCA', *New Zealand Journal of Educational Studies*, 18, 154 – 65

Neale, M.D. (1958) *Neale Analysis of Reading Ability Manual*, Macmillan, London

Newell, P. (1983) *ACE Special Education Handbook*, Advisory Centre for Education, London

Newbold, D.D. (1977) *Ability Grouping — The Banbury Inquiry*, NFER, Windsor

Nias, J. (1980) 'Leadership Styles and Job Satisfaction in Primary Schools', in T. Bush, R. Glatter and C. Riches (eds.), *Approach to School Management*, Harper and Row, London

Osterling, O. (1967) *The Efficacy of Special Education*, Scandinavian University Books, Uppsala

Pidgeon, D.A. (1970) *Expectation and Pupil Performance*, NFER, Windsor

Power, M.J., Alderson, M.R., Phillipson, C.M., Schoenberg, E. and Morris, J.M. (1967) 'Delinquent Schools', *New Society*, 19 October

Power, M.J., Benn, R.T. and Morris, J.M. (1972) 'Neighbourhood, School and Juveniles Before the Courts', *British Journal of Criminology*, 12, 111 – 32

Pratt, J. (1978) 'Perceived Stress Among Teachers: The Effects of Age and Background of Children Taught', *Educational Review*, 30, 3 – 14

Pumfrey, P. (1976) *Reading Tests and Assessment Techniques*, Hodder and Stoughton, London

Rabinowitz, A. (1981) 'The Range of Solutions: A Critical Analysis. in B. Gillham (ed.), *Problem Behaviour in the Secondary School: A Systems Approach*, Croom Helm, London

Reid, N., Jackson, P., Gilmore, A. and Croft, C. (1981) *Test of Scholastic Abilities: Teacher's Manual*, New Zealand Council for Educational Research, Wellington

Reynolds, D. (1976) 'When Pupils and Teachers Refuse a Truce: The Secondary School and the Creation of Delinquency', in G. Mungham and G. Pearson (eds.), *Working Class Youth Culture*, Routledge and Kegan Paul, London

Reynolds, D. (1982) 'The Search for Effective Schools', *School Organisation*, 2, 215 – 37

Reynolds, D. and Murgatroyd, S. (1977) 'The Sociology of Schooling and the Absent Pupils: The School as a Factor in the Generation of Truancy', in H.C.M. Carroll (ed.), *Absenteeism in South Wales: Studies of Pupils, Their Homes and Their Secondary Schools*, University College, Swansea, Faculty of Education, Swansea

Reynolds, D., Jones, S., St. Leger, S. and Murgatroyd, S. (1980) 'School Factors and Truancy', in L. Hersov and I. Berg (eds.), *Out of School: Modern Perspective in Truancy and School Refusal*, Wiley, Chichester

Reynolds, D., St. Leger, S., Jones, D. and Murgatroyd, S. (1985) 'Bringing Schools Back In', (Forthcoming)

Robins, L.N. (1966) *Deviant Children Grown Up*, Williams and Wilkins, Baltimore

Robins, L.N. (1972) 'Follow Up Studies of Behaviour Disorder in Children', in H.C. Quay and J.S. Werry, *Psychopathological Disorders of Childhood*, Wiley, New York

Rogers, C. (1951) *Client Centred Therapy*, Houghton Mifflin, Boston

Rudd, W.G.A. and Wiseman, S. (1962) 'Sources of Dissatisfaction Among a Group of Teachers', *British Journal of Educational Psychology*, 32, 275 – 91

Rutter, M. (1966) *Children of Sick Parents: An Environmental and Psychiatric Study*, Institute of Psychiatry, Maudsley Monographs No 16, Oxford University Press, London

Rutter, M. (1967) 'A Children's Behaviour Questionnaire for Completion by Teachers: Preliminary Findings', *Journal of Child Psychology and Psychiatry*, 8, 1 – 11

Rutter, M. (1977) 'Prospective Studies to Investigate Behavioural Change', in J.S. Strauss, H.M. Babigian and M. Roff (eds.), *Methods of Longitudinal Research in Psychopathology*, Plenum Publishing, New York

Rutter, M. (1978) 'Family, Area and School Influence in the Genesis of Conduct

Disorders', in L. Hersov, M. Berger and D. Schaffer (eds.), *Aggression and Anti-Social Behaviour in Childhood and Adolescence*, Pergamon, Oxford

Rutter, M. and Graham, P. (1968) The Reliability and Validity of the Psychiatric Assessment of the Child: 1. Interview with the Child. *British Journal of Psychiatry*, 114, 563 – 79

Rutter, M., Graham, P., Chadwick, O.F.D. and Yule, W. (1976) Adolescent Turmoil: Fact or Fiction, *Journal of Child Psychology and Psychiatry*, 17, 35 – 56

Rutter, M., Maughan, B., Mortimore, P., Ouston, J. and Smith, A. (1979) *Fifteen Thousand Hours: Secondary Schools and Their Effects on Pupils*, Open Books, London

Rutter, M., Tizard, J. and Whitmore, K. (1970) *Education, Health and Behaviour*, Longman, London

Rutter, M., Yule, B., Quinton, D., Rowlands, O., Yule, W. and Berger, M. (1975) 'Attainments and Adjustment in Two Geographical Areas: III Some Factors Accounting for Area Differences', *British Journal of Psychiatry*, 126, 520 – 33

Sampson, O.C. (1975) *Remedial Education*, Routledge and Kegan Paul, London

Schmidt, G.L. (1976) 'Job Satisfaction Among Secondary School Administrators', *Educational Administration Quarterly*, 12, 68 – 86

Schonell, F.J. and Goodacre, E. (1974) *The Psychology and Teaching of Reading*, Oliver and Boyd, Edinburgh

Scottish Education Department (1978) *The Education of Pupils with Learning Difficulties in Primary and Secondary Schools in Scotland: A Progress Report by Her Majesty's Inspectorate*, HMSO, Edinburgh

Seligman, M.E.P. (1975) *Helplessness: On Depression, Development and Death*, Freeman, San Francisco

Sergiovanni, T. (1967) 'Factors Which Effect Satisfaction and Dissatisfaction of Teachers', *Journal of Educational Administration*, 5, 66 – 82

Sewell, G. (1981) 'The Micro-Sociology of Segregation: Case Studies in the Exclusion of Children with Special Needs from Ordinary Schools, in L. Barton and S. Tomlinson (eds.), *Special Education: Policy, Practices and Social Issues*, Harper and Row, London

Sheffield Psychological Service (1981) *Projects of the Psychological Service*, Sheffield l.e.a. Psychological Service, Sheffield

Simpson, J. (1962) 'Sickness Absence in Teachers', *British Journal of Industrial Medicine*, 19, 110 – 15

Simpson, J. (1976) 'Stress, Sickness Absence and Teachers', in National Association of Schoolmasters and Union of Women Teachers (eds.), *Stress in Schools*, NAS/UWT, Hemel Hempstead

Stott, D.H. (1963) *The Social Adjustment of Children*, 2nd edn, University of London Press, London

Stott, D.H. (1971) *The Bristol Social Adjustment Guides*, University of London Press, London

Strivens, J. (1981) 'The Use of Behaviour Modification in Special Education: A Critique', in L. Barton and S. Tomlinson (eds.), *Special Education: Policy, Practices and Social Issues*, Harper and Row, London

Sutton, A. (1978) Theory, Practice and Cost in Child Care: Implications from an Individual Case, *Howard League Journal*, 16, 159 – 71

Taylor, M., Miller, J. and Oliveira, M. (1979) 'The Off-site Unit', *Comprehensive Education*, 39, 375, 13 – 17

Thompson, D. (1974) 'Non-Streaming Did Make a Difference', *Forum*, 16, 45 – 9

Tizard, J., Schofield, W.N. and Hewison, J. (1982) 'Collaboration Between Teachers and Parents in Assisting Children's Reading', *British Journal of Educational Psychology*, 52, 1 – 15

Tomlinson, S. (1981) *Educational Subnormality: A Study in Decision-Making*, Routledge and Kegan Paul, London

Tomlinson, S. (1982) *The Sociology of Special Education*, Routledge and Kegan Paul, London

Tung, R.L. and Koch, J.L. (1980) School Administrators: Sources of Stress and Ways of Coping With it, in C.L. Cooper and J. Marshal (eds.), *White Collar and Professional Stress*, Wiley, Chichester

Tutt, N. (1981) 'Treatment Under Attack', in B. Gillham (ed.), *Problem Behaviour in the Secondary School*, Croom Helm, London

Uger, C. (1938) 'The Relationship of Teachers' Attitudes to Children's Problem Behaviour', *School and Society*, 47, 246 – 8

United States Statutes (1975) *The Education for all Handicapped Children Act:* Public Law, 94 – 142

Vacc, N.A. (1968) 'A Study of Emotionally Disturbed Children in Regular and Special Classes', *Exceptional Children*, 35, 197 – 204

Vacc, N.A. (1972) 'Long Term Effects of Special Class Intervention for Emotionally Disturbed Children', *Exceptional Children*, 39, 15 – 22

Vetter, E.W. (1976) 'Role Pressure and the School Principal', *National Association of Secondary School Principals Bulletin*, 60, 406, 11 – 23

Wahler, R.G. (1980) 'Behaviour Modification: Application to Childhood Problems', in P. Sholevar, R.M. Benson and B.J. Blinder (eds.) *Emotional Disorders in Children and Adolescents*, MTP Press, Lancaster

Wedge, P. and Essen, J. (1982) *Children in Adversity*, Pan, London

Wedge, P. and Prosser, H. (1973) *Born to Fail?* Arrow Books, London

Welton, J., Wedell, K. and Vorhaus, G. (1982) *Meeting Special Educational Needs: The 1981 Educational Act and its Implications*, Bedford Way Papers 12, Institute of Education, University of London, London

West, D.J. and Farrington, D. (1973) *Who Becomes Delinquent?* Heinemann, London

Wheldall, K. (1982) 'Behavioural Pedagogy or Behavioural Overkill?' *Educational Psychology*, 2, 181 – 4

White, R. and Brockington, D. (1978) *In and Out of School: The ROSLA Community Education Project*, Routledge and Kegan Paul, London

Wilcox, B., and Eustace, P.J. (1980) *Tooling up for Curriculum Review*, NFER, Windsor

Willis, P. (1977) *Learning to Labour: How Working Class Kids Get Working Class Jobs*, Saxon House, Farnborough

Wolcott, H.F. (1973) *The Man in the Principal's Office: An Ethnography*, Holt, Rinehart and Winston, New York

Wolf, M.G. (1970) 'Need Gratification Theory: A Theoretical Reformation of Job Satisfaction/Dissatisfaction and Job Motivation', *Journal of Applied Psychology*, 54, 87 – 94

Wright, D.M., Moelis, I. and Pollack, L.J. (1976) 'The Outcome of Individual

Child Psychotherapy: Increments at Follow-Up', *Journal of Child Psychology and Psychiatry*, 17, 275 – 85

Yule, W. (1973) 'Differential Prognosis of Reading Backwardness and Specific Reading Retardation', *British Journal of Educational Psychology*, 43, 244 – 8

Yule, W. (1976) 'Critical Notice (Taxonomy of Behaviour Disturbance', (ed.), D.H. Stolt, N.C. Marston and S.J. Neill. London: University of London Press) *Therapeutic Education*, 4, 1, 45 – 47

Yule, W., Rutter, M., Berger, M. and Thompson, J. (1974) 'Over- and Under-Achievement in Reading: Distribution in the General Population', *British Journal of Educational Psychology*, 44, 1 – 12

INDEX